S0-ACH-100

Sadlier

CHRIST IN US ™

Parish Edition 2

"*Christ In Us* Grade 2 cover artwork speaks to the children's discovery of the joys of exploring the believing community."

Reverend Donald Senior, C.P., S.T.D.

S ® **Sadlier Religion**

This advanced publication copy has been printed prior to final publication and pending ecclesiastical approval.

Acknowledgments

This publication was printed with permission pending from the following copyright holders.

Excerpts from the *Catechism of the Catholic Church, second edition,* © 2000, Libreria Editrice Vaticana—United States Conference of Catholic Bishops, Washington, D.C. All rights reserved.

Scripture texts in this work are taken from the *New American Bible,* revised edition © 2010, 1991, 1986, 1970 Confraternity of Christian Doctrine, Washington, D.C. All Rights Reserved. No part of the *New American Bible* may be reproduced in any form without permission in writing from the copyright owner.

Excerpts from the English translation of *The Roman Missal* © 2010 International Commission on English in the Liturgy, Inc. (ICEL). All rights reserved.

Excerpts from the *Lectionary for Mass for Use in the Dioceses of the United States of America, second typical edition* © 2001, 1998, 1997, 1986, 1970 Confraternity of Christian Doctrine, Inc., Washington, D.C. All rights reserved. No portion of this text may be reproduced by any means without permission in writing from the copyright owner.

Excerpts from the English translation of *Rite of Penance* © 1974, International Committee on English in the Liturgy, Inc. All rights reserved.

Excerpts from *The Order of Confirmation.* Copyright © 2016, United States Conference of Catholic Bishops, Inc., Washington, D.C. All rights reserved.

Quotations from papal addresses, audiences, homilies, speeches, messages, meditations, encyclicals, and other Vatican documents are from www.vatican.va and copyright © by Libreria Editrice Vaticana.

English translation of the Glory to the Father, Apostles' Creed, Nicene Creed, Lord's Prayer and Gloria in Excelsis by the International Consultation on English Texts (ICET).

Excerpts from *Catholic Household Blessings and Prayers (Revised Edition)* © 1988, 2007, United States Catholic Conference, Inc. Washington, D.C. All rights reserved.

Excerpt from Thomas McNally, C.S.C., and William George Storey, D.M.S., Editors, *Day by Day: The Notre Dame Prayer Book* for Students, Ave Maria Press, Notre Dame, IN, 1975. Copyright © 1975 by Ave Maria Press.

Excerpts from *Saints for Sinners,* by Alban Goodier, S.J., © 1959, Image Books: A Division of Doubleday & Company, Inc., New York, NY by special arrangement with Sheed & Ward, Inc.

Excerpts from "O Come, O Come, Emanuel" GIA music. © 1996 by GIA Publications, Inc., 7404 S. Mason Ave., Chicago, IL 60638 • www.giamusic.com • 800.442.1358. All rights reserved. Excerpts from "Hark! the Herald Angels Sing" GIA music. © 2018 by GIA Publications, Inc., 7404 S. Mason Ave., Chicago, IL 60638 • www.giamusic.com • 800.442.1358. All rights reserved.

Copyright © 2020 by William H. Sadlier, Inc. All rights reserved. This book, or any part thereof, may not be reproduced in any form, or by any means, including electronic, photographic, or mechanical, or by any sound recording system, or by any device for storage and retrieval of information, without the written permission of the publisher.

Printed in the United States of America.

S® and Sadlier Religion® are registered trademarks of William H. Sadlier, Inc. All rights reserved.

CHRIST IN US™ is a trademark of William H. Sadlier, Inc.

William H. Sadlier, Inc.
9 Pine Street
New York, NY 10005-4700

ISBN: 978-0-8215-3692-6
123456789 WEBC 23 22 21 20 19

Cover Series Design: Silver Linings Studios. **Cover Series Illustrator:** Jui Ishida.

Photo Credits

age fotostock: 223; Annie Engel: 149; Blend Images/Hill Street Studios: 93; Blend Images/KidStock: 195; Hero Images: 77, 106; Hero Images/Drew Myers: 105; Hill Street Studios: 126; Superstock: 146; Syda Productions: 115; UIG/Godong: 207; VStock LLC: 43. Alamy Stock Photo/Ian Allenden: 268; Stephen Barnes: 79; James Boardman: 157; Marin Bulat: 249; Tom Carter: 108; Lev Dolgachov: 114; Ted Foxx: 24 *right*; Norma Jean Gargasz: 137; Myrleen Pearson: 64, 131, 240 *bottom*, 250, 251; Adrian Sherratt: 180; Peter Treanor: 73 *top right*; Borderlands: 73 *bottom right*; christitzeimaging.com: 31; Godong: 73 *left*; Godong/Photononstop: 80, 213; Image Source/Wonwoo Lee: 145; M.T.M. Images: 69; Torontonian: 24 *left*, 245; Zoonar GmbH/Olga Altunina: 226–227 *bottom*. Associated Press/Vatican Media L'Osservatore Romano/Pool Photo: 56. Bridgeman Images: 209 *bottom*; Ashmolean Museum, University of Oxford, UK: 136; Look and Learn/Elgar Collection: 172; Prismatic Pictures/Kykkos Monastery, Cyprus: 23. Karen Callaway: 63, 78, 258, 260, 264, 266.

Corbis/Wavebreak Media LTD: 87. The Crosiers/Gene Plaisted, OSC: 27, 32, 53; 40, 45, 48, 61, 241, 262, 265. Eyekons/The Last Supper © 2016 John August Swanson: 82.

Fotolia.com/bonniemarie: 47; kot500: 104. Getty Images/choja: 128; marabird: 37; Stefan Cristian Cioata: 203 *top*; Sebastien Desarmaux: 130; J. Emilio Flores: 62; Ken Hively: 163; Ariel Skelley: 54, 178; AFP/Molly Riley: 111; Andersen Ross Productions/Amy Andersen & Jonathan Ross: 98; Blend Images/KidStock: 138 *top*, 182; Brand X Pictures: 229; Corbis/VCG/Beau Lark: 174; Jamie Grill Photography: 200; Jupiterimages: 164; NurPhoto/Massimo Valicchia: 124; Stockbyte: 113 *top*; VCG/Corbis/Jose Luis Pelaez: 116. GoodSalt/Lars Justinen: 154; Jeff Preston: 201; Lifeway Collection: 191 *bottom*; Providence Collection: 90, 147, 150, 219, 233 *center*.

iStockphoto.com/AlexmarPhoto: 202–203 *bottom*; bgphoto: 230; borchee: 194; cstar55: 140; D-Keine: 211; davex83: 97; DGLimages: 119; FatCamera: 6, 28, 135,148, 156, 158, 170; gradyreece: 112; Imgorthand: 103; ithinksky: 196–197 *bottom*; joshblake: 217; kali9: 122; Kozlik_Mozlik: 215 *bottom*; KristianSeptimiusKrogh: 197 *top*; laflor: 173; Linleo: 171; Lisa-Blue: 127; ManoAfrica: 74; michaeljung: 85; naumoid: 205; pepifoto: 206; Smileus: 46; stellalevi: 212; VikahSuh: 243; yupiyan: 153; Steve Debenport: 181; Thomas Soellner: 21; GlobalStock: 129; MPKphotos: 193; MStudioImages: 35 Valenaphoto: 139. Masterfile: 19. Newscom/Design Pics: 221 *top*; Polaris/CPP/OR: 51.

Shutterstock.com/arapix: 12; buchan: 236 *top*, 237 *top*; ESB Professional: 11; hydebrink: 189; IgorZh: 224; JmeL: 132; logoboom: 179; Macrovector: 190–191 *top*, 208–209 *top*, 214–215 *top*, 232–233 *top*; Permaphoto: 66; piosi: 227 *top*; pixfly: 107; Pressmaster: 113 *bottom*; Redcollegiya: i, 196–197 *background*, 202–203 *background*, 220–221 *background*, 226–227 *background*, 235; sakkmesterke: 238; Slanapotam: 18 *background*, 60 *background*, 102 *background*, 144 *background*, 186 *background*; studiogi: 199; Tashsat: 247; Thoom: 72, 225; Triff: 187; Wendy Corniquet: 29; Svetlana Danilova: 218; R. Daniluk: 244; Nataliya Dolotko: 235; Howard Grill: 220–221 *bottom*; Chen Heng Kong: 236 *bottom*, 237 *bottom*; Romolo Tavani: 242; Terrie L. Zeller: 231; Africa Studio: 269; LightField Studios: 155; MIA Studio: 166; Monkey Business Images: 138 *bottom*; Rawpixel.com: 121, 165; SP-Photo: 188; wavebreakmedia: 14, 86. Spirit Juice Studios: 70, 88, 89, 177, 256, 259, 267. Stockbyte: 169. SuperStock/ACME Imagery: 20; Asia Images/Alex Mares-Manton: 161; Exactostock/George Doyle: 123; Exactostock-1598/Paul Burns: 38; F1 ONLINE/Jürgen Ritterbach: 252–253; Purestock/Lissette LeBon: 36. W.P. Wittman Ltd: 7, 52, 65, 71, 81, 94, 95, 96, 257, 261, 263. Wikimedia: 44, 55, 246..

Illustrator Credits

Sally Wern Comport: 10, 13, 25, 33, 41, 49, 57, 67, 75, 83, 91, 99, 109, 117, 125, 133, 141, 151, 159, 167, 175, 183. Robert Kayganich: 254-255. Jim Madsen: 271, 272, 273, 274. David Sossella: 22, 30, 39, 47, 50, 53, 98, 110, 142, 160, 164, 224. Gerad Taylor: 248. Scott Wakefield: 17, 59, 101, 143.

Christ In Us was developed in collaboration with the wisdom of the community. The team included respected catechetical, liturgical, pastoral, and theological experts who shared their insights and inspired its development.

With grateful acknowledgment of
William Sadlier Dinger and Frank Sadlier Dinger
for their leadership, vision, and commitment to excellence in the development
of Sadlier's catechetical programs and resources since 1963

Theological and Liturgical Consultants

Most Reverend Christopher James Coyne
Bishop of Burlington, VT

Donna Eschenauer, Ph.D.
Associate Dean, Associate Professor of
    Pastoral Theology
St. Joseph's Seminary and College

Rita Ferrone, M.Div.

Thomas Kendzia
Sadlier National Consultant for
    Liturgy and Music

Reverend Monsignor John Pollard, M.Ed., S.T.L.

Alissa Thorell, M.T.S.

John B. Angotti, M.A.P.S.

Barbara Sutton, D.Min.

Kathleen Dorsey Bellow, D.Min.

Scripture Consultant

Reverend Donald Senior, C.P., S.T.D.
Chancellor and President Emeritus
Catholic Theological Union

Catechetical Consultants

Amy Welborn, M.A.

Susan Stark

Sr. Theresa Engel, O.S.F.
Member of the School Sisters of St. Francis

Maureen A. Kelly, M.A.

Karla Manternach, M.A.

Woodeene Koenig-Bricker, M.A.

Connie Clark

Shannon Chisholm, Ph.D.

Susan M. Sink

Maureen Shaughnessy, S.C.

Lori Dahlhoff, Ed.D.

Andrea D. Chavez-Kopp, M.Ed.

Educational Consultants

Richard Culatta

Heidi Hayes Jacobs, Ed.D.

Jay McTighe

Allie Johnston

Learning Style Inclusion Consultants

Charleen Katra, M.A.

Jennifer Ochoa, M.Ed., LDT/C

Inculturation Consultants

Luis J. Medina
Director, Bilingual Catechesis

Charlene Howard, M.A.

Michael P. Howard, M.A.
Eat the Scroll Ministry

Catholic Social Teaching

Kristin Witte, D.Min.

Genevieve Jordan Laskey, M.A.

Michael Jordan Laskey, M.A.

Media and Technology Consultants

Spirit Juice Studios

Top Floor Productions

Sr. Caroline Cerveny, S.S.J.-T.O.S.F., D.Min.

Reviewers and Contributors

Jennifer Hayhurst

Concetta M. Duval, Ed.D.

Trenton W. Mattingly, M.A.

Debi Mahr, M.A.

Mary Homola, M.A.

Linda Mele Dougherty, M.A.

Mary Jane Krebbs, Ph.D.

Darcy Osby, M.Div.

Hugh M. Keenan

Sadlier Consultant Team

Steven Botsford
Senior Director of Digital Catechesis

Suzan Larroquette, M.T.S.
Senior Director of Catechetical Consultant Services

Kathleen Hendricks, M.A.
National Catechetical Consultant
Contributing Writer

John Collins, M.Ed.
National Religion Consultant

Writing/Development Team

Diane Lampitt, M.Ed.
Vice President, Product Manager, Religion

Blake Bergen
Vice President, Religion Editorial

Deacon Matthew Halbach, Ph.D.
Senior Catechetical Director

Regina Kelly, M.A.
Editorial Director, Religion

Gloria Shahin, M.A.
Senior Editorial Director, Religion

Mary Carol Kendzia, M.S.
Research and Development Director, Religion

Robert Vigneri, M.S.
Executive Editor, Religion

Editorial Staff

Tina Dennelly, Linda Nicholson, Roger Ochoa, Amanda Pisciotta

Publishing Operations Team

Patricia Coryell
Senior Vice President & Publisher

Kevin Feyen
Vice President, Shared Services

Carole Uettwiller
Vice President, Supply Chain

Vince Gallo
Senior Creative Director

Francesca O'Malley
Art/Design Director

Cesar Llacuna
Senior Image Manager

Roderick Gammon
Senior Director, Digital Strategy

Toby Carson
Digital Design Director

Cheryl Golding
Senior Production Director

Laura Reischour
Project Manager

Evie Alvarez
Program Manager

Jovito Pagkalinawan
Electronic Prepress Director

Yolanda Miley
Image Rights & Permissions Director

Lucy Rotondi
Business Manager

Design/Image Staff
Kevin Butler, Nancy Figueiredo, Stephen Flanagan, Debrah Kaiser, Gabriel Ricci, Bob Schatz, Daniel Sherman

Production Staff
Robin D'Amato, Carol Lin, Vincent McDonough, Allison Pagkalinawan, Brad Tucker

Contents

Your Spiritual Journey

Christ In Us offers a saint for every grade. As you journey through each unit, remember to pray to your grade's saint. Ask him or her to help guide you to be closer to Jesus Christ.

Saint Thérèse was born in 1873 into a kind and loving Catholic family.

Thérèse was a happy little girl. She loved to laugh. She wanted to do great things in life. She was known as the "Little Flower."

Gradually, Thérèse's love of Jesus grew and grew. She wanted to be a nun. She wanted to do great things as a nun.

Thérèse entered the convent. She was not happy at first. Where were the "great things" to do in life?

But gradually Thérèse felt a simple love and devotion to God. She saw in every little action in life a way to love God. She saw in every person a way to show love for God.

Doing great things might be fine. But finding God's love in all the ordinary moments in the day fills the heart. We call this Thérèse's "little way."

Where will you find God's love today?

Welcome to **Christ In Us**, an exciting way to grow in your Catholic faith!

Each one of us is on a journey to love and know Jesus Christ. Imagine if every person who met you also met Christ in you!

Together in this program, we will

ENCOUNTER Jesus Christ

ACCOMPANY each other as we learn our Catholic faith

WITNESS to our faith.

You will use this book as well as your online digital portal as you discover and grow closer to Jesus Christ.

As you journey in your faith, you can think about these questions:

"It is Christ in you; the hope for glory."
Colossians 1:27

What would happen if you did not have Jesus in your life?

Why is it important to have Christ live in you?

How does your faith, the Church, and your family help bring you closer to God?

Every lesson has four Spiraling Main Ideas.
Here is an example.

Faith Words in the lessons help you to understand the important words we use as Catholics.

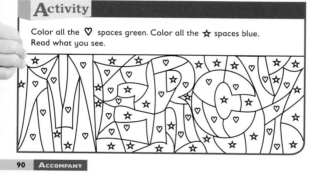

God shows his mercy and love in the Sacrament of Penance.

When we celebrate the Sacrament of Penance, we receive God's forgiveness and peace. We are at peace with God and one another. We are forgiven for our sins.

Another word for God's love and forgiveness is **mercy**. God will always forgive us when we are sorry.

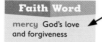

Faith Word

mercy God's love and forgiveness

"And when he does find it, he sets it on his shoulders with great joy and, upon his arrival home, he calls together his friends and neighbors and says to them, 'Rejoice with me because I have found my lost sheep.'" Luke 15:5–6

Activity

Color all the ♡ spaces green. Color all the ☆ spaces blue. Read what you see.

90 ACCOMPANY

Be sure to look at all the wonderful photos and beautiful art on the pages of your book.

As you explore this question, you might be asked to stop and think more about it and then do a short **Activity** to answer it better.

You will be asked to **Show What You Know** by writing the answers to some short questions pertaining to the lesson.

You will not be alone as you journey through **Christ In Us**. You will have a lot of **Partners in Faith**—saints and other holy people who lived amazing lives—walking with you.

Along with Saint Thérèse of Lisieux, here are some other Partners in Faith whom you will meet throughout the book!

Saint Patrick

Saint Elizabeth

Saint Juan Diego

Saint Teresa of Calcutta

Saint Paul

Saint Catherine of Siena

Saint Ignatius of Antioch

Saint Bernadette Soubirous

Next, you will be asked to go to your **Portfolio** to creatively share how you can bring Christ to the world.

Each lesson ends with a **Mini-Task** that invites you to show ways you can live out your faith as a missionary disciple of Christ.

Finally, you will be given ways to think and talk with your family **At Home**.

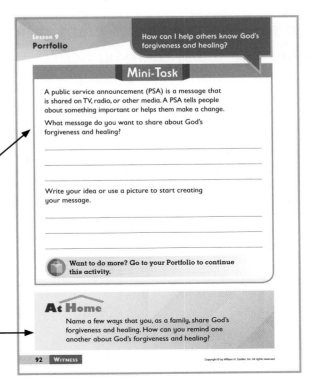

Lesson 9
Portfolio

How can I help others know God's forgiveness and healing?

Mini-Task

A public service announcement (PSA) is a message that is shared on TV, radio, or other media. A PSA tells people about something important or helps them make a change.

What message do you want to share about God's forgiveness and healing?

Write your idea or use a picture to start creating your message.

Want to do more? Go to your Portfolio to continue this activity.

At Home

Name a few ways that you, as a family, share God's forgiveness and healing. How can you remind one another about God's forgiveness and healing?

92 WITNESS

Copyright © by William H. Sadlier, Inc. All rights reserved.

Christ In Us features an online portal filled with exciting media and activities to go with the lessons in your book. If you see one of these icons below in your book, you know it's time to visit the student portal for more. (Note: Not every icon will appear in your book.)

Participate in lesson prayers, whose words are online and downloadable.

Learn more about the lesson's **Did You Know?** topic by watching an interesting video and doing an activity.

Learn more about the lesson's **Partner in Faith** by watching an online video and completing the activity that follows.

Listen to Scripture verses and Catholic prayers and learn them by heart.

Find fun activities to share and recall what you have learned.

Show What You Know by completing online assessments.

Read and remember the **Faith Words** definitions.

Complete projects and tasks in the online **Portfolio** or *Portfolio Workbook*.

Listen to the songs for your grade level and sing along!

Your Songs for Grade 2	
Unit Songs	**Liturgical Catechesis Seasonal Songs**
Unit 1: "In My Heart," Spiritual	**Advent:** "O Come, O Come, Emmanuel"
Unit 2: "Light Of Christ," Tom Kendzia/OCP	**Christmas:** "Silent Night"
Unit 3: "Prayer of St. Francis," Sebastian Temple/OCP	**Easter:** "Over My Head," Tom Kendzia/OCP, Spiritual
Unit 4: "We Are Marching," African Traditional	**Pentecost:** "Go Out, Go Out," Curtis Stephan/OCP
Unit 5: "We Will Praise You," Tom Kendzia/OCP	

Become a "digital disciple"!

The **Christ In Us** online portal allows you to explore all the exciting resources that blend together with your textbook.

Take a look at your personalized online dashboard. Everything you need is at your fingertips!

- Think of your portfolio as your digital backpack! Here you can get your assignments, see reminders, send emails, and even talk to your catechist.

- With the interactive Mini-Tasks you will be able to share exciting activities with others. You will be able to get hands-on and creative by making videos or interactive posters.

- Listen with your heart and pray the prayers of *Lectio* and *Visio Divina*, praise, thanksgiving, intercession, adoration, and petition from your lesson.

- Track your progress with digital quizzes and tests.

Have a wonderful year!

What do we believe?

Unit 1
The Faith Professed

The Annunciation

Unit Prayer

Leader: The Little Flower, Saint Thérèse of Lisieux, loved Jesus very much. She felt that the Church was like a mother to her and a sign of Jesus' great love for the world.

Let us listen to how Jesus' love is made known to us today in the world. Listen to the stories of missionary disciples in our midst.

Let us pray:
Jesus, we see your love in the Mass, in the sacraments, and in the lives of those who shared their stories today. For these great gifts, we pray in thanksgiving.

Reader: For the gift of the Church,

All: we thank you, Jesus.

Reader: For the gift of the Mass,

All: we thank you, Jesus.

Reader: For the gift of the sacraments,

All: we thank you, Jesus.

Reader: With Saint Thérèse, we say: "Jesus, my love!"

All: Jesus, my love!

All sing: "In My Heart"

 Unit Song: "In My Heart," Spiritual

Missionary Discipleship

Think about a time when you experienced the love of Jesus. What happened? How did you feel? Did you celebrate this experience?

How do we know God?

God loves us. He knows everything about us. God wants us to know him, too. How do we come to know God? In many ways! We learn about God most fully from Jesus. We also learn about God from the Bible, the Church, and creation. They teach us about God's love and about his promise to love us forever.

 Go to the digital portal for a *Lectio* and *Visio Divina* prayer.

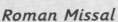

"I believe in one God,
the Father almighty,
maker of heaven and earth,
of all things visible and invisible."

Roman Missal

> "Then the angel said to her, 'Do not be afraid, Mary, for you have found favor with God.'"
>
> Luke 1:30

We learn about God's love.

How can you tell when people love you? Maybe they take care of you or spend time with you. God loves us, too. He promises to love us forever.

We learn about God's love in many ways. Look around! God made the world so we would know his goodness and love. God showed his love for us the most by sending us his divine Son, Jesus.

God sent an angel to visit a young woman named Mary. Angels are spiritual beings that God created. They do not have a body as humans do. They give glory to God. They are also messengers of God.

What do I know about God?

Did You Know?

 Monks copied the first Bibles by hand.

The Bible teaches us about God's promises.

God did not leave us alone to come to know him. He tells us in the Bible about himself and his love. The Bible is the book that contains his own Word.

God gave the writers of the Bible a gift to help them write it. The Holy Spirit, the Third Person of the Blessed Trinity, helped them so we could come to know and love God.

Faith Word

covenant an agreement between God and his people

The Bible tells us that God made a **covenant**, or an agreement, between himself and his people. In this covenant, God promised to love us forever. We would be his people, and he would be our God.

The most important writings in the Bible are about God's divine Son, Jesus. Jesus teaches us how much God loves us. Jesus also teaches us that God wants us to love each other. Jesus fully shows us who God is because he is the Son of God.

Activity

God gives us many gifts. Use the word list to circle some of God's gifts. Which gift is the most important? Color it yellow. Tell a friend why God's gifts are inside a heart.

Word List

BIBLE
CHURCH
CREATION
JESUS
WORLD

```
      L C           B W
    Y F Y P       M I O G
  M C H U R C H B R V H
  V U A W G R K L L J A
  J E S U S E M E D K B
  Q N N E A K C H K
    D S Y T E W D
      I F I V V
      X O Y
        N
```

Jesus' life shows us God's love.

God's love for us is enormous. It is like a mountain so high that nobody can ever climb to the top. It is like an ocean so deep that nobody can ever swim to the bottom.

God's love is too great for us to imagine! That is why Jesus was born. Jesus is the divine Son of God. Jesus is God himself telling us how much he loves us.

Jesus showed his Father's love in many ways. Jesus helped people. He healed the sick. He comforted people who were sad. All these things show us how much God loves and cares for us.

Jesus also taught us to love other people. He showed us how God wants us to act. Jesus helped us get to know God better by everything he said and did. Jesus, the Son of God, born of the Virgin Mary, showed us how to love God more and more.

Activity

Jesus wanted children to come to him. He taught them about God's love. Draw yourself with Jesus. Tell a friend what you imagine Jesus is saying to you.

The Church teaches and shares Jesus' message of God's love.

Jesus chose the **Apostles** to continue his work after he died. These twelve men were chosen by Jesus to lead his disciples. The first Apostles spent time with Jesus and followed him because he was the Son of God.

Faith Word

Apostles the twelve men that Jesus chose to lead his disciples

Jesus is still with us today. He sent his Apostles to tell the world about his Father's love. They passed on what Jesus said and did. The Church calls this Sacred Tradition. Sacred Tradition and Scripture tell us the truth about Jesus.

 Apostles' Creed

The **Church** is founded on Jesus, his grace, and his teachings, which his Apostles received and handed down to their successors, the bishops.

The Church is a community of people who believe that Jesus is the Son of God. Jesus is the Head of the Church. The Church includes those who, through faith and Baptism, follow the teachings of Jesus and are governed by the bishops in union with the pope. The pope and the bishops guide us in our understanding of Sacred Scripture and Tradition. They are known as the Magisterium, or the teaching office of the Church.

Faith Word

Church all the people who are baptized in the name of the Blessed Trinity and are part of the Body of Christ

Through Sacred Scripture and Tradition, the Church's Magisterium teaches the message of God's love and shares it with others. We are a part of the Church. We can all help share God's love with others!

Faith Words

covenant   Church   Apostles

 Show What You Know

Complete the sentences with the correct Faith Word.

1. God made a _____ with his people, promising to love them forever.

2. Jesus chose twelve _____ to lead his followers.

3. The _____ is all the people who are baptized in Jesus Christ and are part of the Body of Christ.

Partners in Faith

Saint Thérèse of Lisieux

Saint Thérèse of Lisieux is called the "Little Flower." She said that we do not have to do big things for God. If we do little things with love, God is happy.

 Learn more about the life of Saint Thérèse of Lisieux.

Copyright © by William H. Sadlier, Inc. All rights reserved.

How do I help others know God?

Mini-Task

One of the ways we learn about God is in the Bible. We can share what we have learned about God's love with others in creative ways.

Jesus shared God's love. Jesus helped people. He healed people who were sick. He comforted sad people.

Draw a picture of Jesus showing God's love.

Share your picture with the group. Tell the others about what you are showing in your picture.

 Want to do more? Go to your Portfolio to continue this activity.

At Home

God always keeps his promises. How can you and others in your family keep your promises? What happens if a promise is broken?

Copyright © by William H. Sadlier, Inc. All rights reserved.

God is our Creator. He made us because of his great love. God always wants to share his love. God gives us many gifts to show his love. He gives us creation. He gives us the Bible and the Church.

The greatest gift is Jesus. Jesus is God the Son, who was sent by the Father. Jesus shows us who the Father is. The Holy Spirit helps us and guides us to live as Jesus showed us, to live as children of God.

Go to the digital portal for a traditional prayer.

"Know that the LORD is God,
he made us, we belong to him."
Psalm 100:3

Jesus is the divine Son of God.

God created us. He did this without any help.

God the Father sent us his only begotten Son, Jesus, to be born of Mary. Jesus is the divine Son of God. God the Father did not create Jesus. Together with the Father and the Holy Spirit, Jesus is God. He is the Son of God in a unique way.

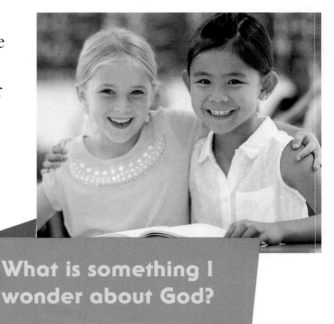

God is loving and gives us love. Jesus taught us to love each other just as God himself loves us. Everything Jesus did and said shows us even more how loving and giving God is!

What is something I wonder about God?

Did You Know?

We mark ourselves with the Sign of the Cross.

Activity

God gives us many gifts. Write the names of some gifts God has given you.

The Blessed Trinity is One God in Three Persons: God the Father, God the Son, and God the Holy Spirit.

Faith Word

Blessed Trinity
One God in Three Persons: God the Father, God the Son, and God the Holy Spirit

There is One God. He has taught us about himself. He has shown us that he is Father, Son, and Holy Spirit. We call this the **Blessed Trinity**. The Blessed Trinity is the Three Persons in One God: God the Father, God the Son, and God the Holy Spirit. The Three Persons of the Blessed Trinity are unique but are one and the same God.

God loves us. God himself is love. The Blessed Trinity shows us the perfect example of love. From this love we learn how to live as Catholics. Our belief in the Blessed Trinity is the center of our whole lives as Catholics.

Activity

There are things in our world that remind us of God the Father, the Son, and the Holy Spirit. Write or draw something that reminds you of each Person of the Blessed Trinity. Choose one of your responses to share with a friend.

> Reminder of God the Father:

> Reminder of God the Son:

> Reminder of God the Holy Spirit:

We cannot fully understand the Blessed Trinity because God will always be greater than our understanding. No matter how much we learn, we will never know everything there is to know about God! The **Sign of the Cross** is a prayer that shows our faith in God, the Blessed Trinity. Every time we pray the Sign of the Cross, we name the Three Persons in One God. We begin and end our prayers by blessing ourselves and saying the name of the One God. We say: "In the name of the Father, and of the Son, and of the Holy Spirit."

Faith Word

Sign of the Cross a blessing prayer of the Church that shows our faith in God, the Blessed Trinity

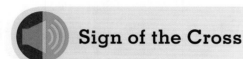

Sign of the Cross

Activity

Trace the lines to make the Sign of the Cross. Now teach a friend to make the Sign of the Cross.

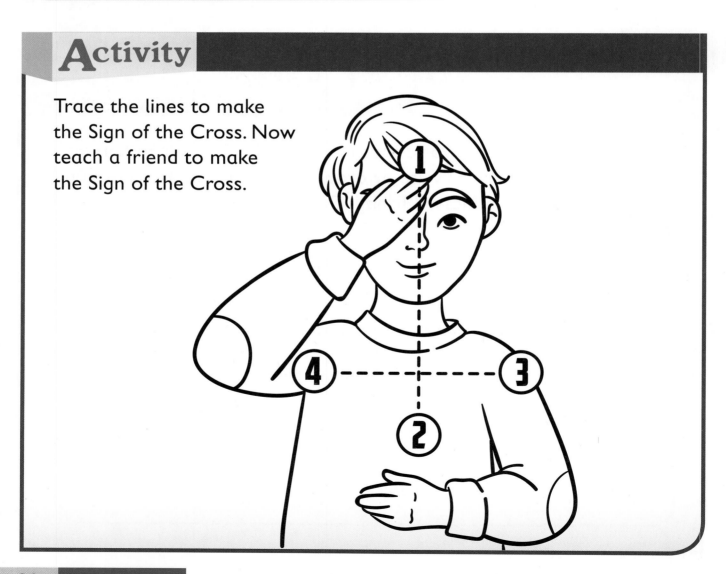

Jesus Christ is the Second Person of the Blessed Trinity.

The Bible tells a story about the first people God made, Adam and Eve. God loved them. Tempted by the Devil, Adam and Eve ate the fruit of the Tree of the Knowledge of Good and Evil, although God told them not to do it. They disobeyed God. They committed a **sin**. The Church calls this act of disobedience the Original Sin. As children of Adam and Eve, all human beings are born with Original Sin. But God promised to send someone to help people turn back to God. He kept that promise by sending Jesus.

Faith Words

sin something we freely choose to do even though we know it is wrong

Christ the title given to Jesus that means he was God's chosen one

Jesus is the only divine Son of God. He is God. He is the Second Person of the Blessed Trinity. God sent Jesus to save us. Jesus helps us turn back to God. The name *Jesus* means "God saves."

God made us because he loves us. God loves us so much that he also sent Jesus to save us from sin. God sent Jesus so we could live in his friendship forever.

We also call Jesus **Christ**. *Christ* means "the chosen one of God, or the one anointed by God." God chose to send Jesus Christ as part of his promise to love us always.

The Holy Spirit is the Third Person of the Blessed Trinity.

Every Sunday at Mass, we pray these words from the Nicene Creed:

> I believe in the Holy Spirit, the Lord, the giver of life.

The Holy Spirit is the Third Person of the Blessed Trinity. God the Father sends us his Son, Jesus, and the Holy Spirit.

The Blessed Trinity, God the Father, God the Son, and God the Holy Spirit, is at work in our lives. God is always with us. We can pray to God, as Father, Son, and Holy Spirit, for help whenever we need it.

God the Father; God the Son, Jesus; and God the Holy Spirit are always with the Church. Christ is the Head of the Church, and the Church is his Body. The Holy Spirit strengthens and guides the Church.

 Breastplate of Saint Patrick

Faith Words

Blessed Trinity	**Sign of the Cross**
sin	**Christ**

 Show What You Know

Circle the correct answers.

1. A blessing prayer of the Church that shows our faith in God, the Blessed Trinity, is the _____.

Stations of the Cross | Sign of the Cross

2. The Blessed Trinity is One God in Three _____.

Persons | Parts

3. When the first people disobeyed God, they committed a _____.

sacrifice | sin

4. Jesus is also called _____.

Christ | Blessed Trinity

Partners in Faith

Saint Patrick was a priest. He lived a long time ago in Ireland. He taught people about the Blessed Trinity. He helped them to believe in One God in Three Persons, the Blessed Trinity.

 Learn more about the life of Saint Patrick.

Copyright © by William H. Sadlier, Inc. All rights reserved.

Mini-Task

A triangle can help remind us of the Blessed Trinity as Three Persons in One God.

Trace the triangle on this page with your finger.

How many sides does it have? _____

How many Persons are in the Blessed Trinity? _____

Label each side of the triangle with the name of one Person of the Blessed Trinity. In the middle of the triangle, write *God*.

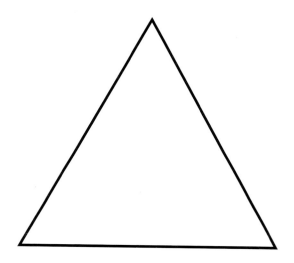

How does the triangle you just made remind you of the Blessed Trinity?

Turn and talk about your triangle with a partner.

 Want to do more? Go to your Portfolio to continue this activity.

At Home

Christ means "chosen one, or anointed one, of God." Discuss the meaning of names in your family. Why were you given your name?

Copyright © by William H. Sadlier, Inc. All rights reserved.

Why did God make us?

Ⓖod is our Creator. He is good and loving. God made us to share in his goodness and love. God wants us to share in his love and life forever. God the Father wants us to know and trust in his love as Jesus taught us. Jesus teaches us how to trust in the Father's love.

Go to the digital portal for a prayer of praise.

"God created mankind in his image;
in the image of God he created them;
male and female he created them."

Genesis 1:27

All creation shares in the goodness of God.

God the Creator is good. The Bible tells us that God created everything out of nothing. God created every person. All of creation shows that God is good.

God made people to be the most like him. He made us to be good and loving. God made us to live with him forever.

What are some ways I share in the goodness of God?

Did You Know?

People are God's most loved creations.

"Blessed are those who trust in the LORD; . . . .
They are like a tree planted beside the waters
that stretches out its roots to the stream:
It does not fear heat when it comes,
its leaves stay green;
In the year of drought it shows no distress,
but still produces fruit."

Jeremiah 17:7–8

Faith helps us to trust in God and his Word to us.

The Bible says that someone who trusts in God is like a tree. Trees are strong, even in a storm. Trees draw water from deep in the earth, even when there has been no rain.

Our faith in God makes us strong, too. Faith is a gift God gives us.

Faith helps us to believe in God and to trust in his love. We trust that God will help us through hard times. Faith helps us remember that God loves us no matter what.

God wants us to know him better. Having faith means learning from God and believing in him and all he has told us. We learn the most about God from his Son, Jesus. We learn about God from the Bible and the Church. Faith is a wonderful gift!

God wants us to trust in him. He is the One, True God. God made us, and we trust that he wants what is good for us. We believe and trust in God alone.

Activity

When we trust God, we are like a strong tree. Complete the following sentences.

When I trust God, I do not fear _____.

When I believe in God, I _____.

When I know God loves me, I am able to _____.

I draw strength from God when I _____.

Jesus shows us the way to trust God.

Sometimes we do not show our love for God. We do what we know God does not want us to do. We sin. When that happens, God wants us to try again. As long as we are sorry and ask his forgiveness, God will forgive us and give us another chance. We must also tell God we will try not to sin again.

God wants us to do our best. He wants us to live as his children. God wants us to trust in his love the way Jesus did.

Activity

We all make bad choices sometimes. We call these "sins." God forgives our sins when we ask him to. Put the letter of each step to forgiveness in the proper order on the path.

A. Do better.   **B.** Ask God to forgive.
C. Be forgiven.   **D.** Make a bad choice.   **E.** Be sorry.
F. Thank God.   **G.** Tell God you are sorry.

Jesus' Resurrection makes possible eternal life with God.

After Jesus was born, he lived for about thirty years. Jesus lived a life in the world just as we do, except without sin. Everything Jesus did, he did out of love. He taught people about God. He helped and healed people. Then Jesus died on the Cross. His followers buried him in a tomb.

After Jesus died, something wonderful happened: Jesus rose from the dead! The Risen Jesus Christ visited his followers. They saw Jesus, touched him, and spoke with him. Jesus was alive!

Jesus' rising from the dead three days after he died is called the **Resurrection**. Now Jesus lives with his Father forever.

God wants *us* to live with him forever, too. He wants us to have **eternal life**. Eternal life is living forever with God in the happiness of heaven.

Jesus died and rose to bring us new life. God promises to love us always. He wants us to live as his friends now so that we can live as his friends forever. One day, God will raise our bodies to new life after we die.

Faith Words

Resurrection **eternal life**

 Show What You Know

Match the terms to their meanings.

1. eternal life

Jesus' rising from the dead

2. faith

living forever with God in the happiness of heaven

3. Resurrection

believing and trusting in God

Complete the sentences.

4. God wants us to _____ in his love as Jesus did.

5. God made us to be _____ and loving.

Partners in Faith

Saint Leo the Great

Attila the Hun wanted to take over Rome with his army. Saint Leo the Great had faith that God would protect the city. He faced Attila, and Attila backed down. The city was saved.

 Learn more about the life of Saint Leo the Great.

Copyright © by William H. Sadlier, Inc. All rights reserved.

Lesson 3
Portfolio

How do I trust in God?

Mini-Task

In this lesson, you read from the Bible that people who trust in God are like a tree planted beside the waters.

> Blessed are those who trust in the LORD; . . .
> They are like a tree planted beside the waters
>   that stretches out its roots to the stream:
> It does not fear heat when it comes,
>   its leaves stay green;
> In the year of drought it shows no distress,
>   but still produces fruit. (Jeremiah 17:7–8)

What do people who trust in God and a tree beside the waters have in common? Share your ideas with your group.

Now, write your own ideas about trusting in God.
Finish the thought below.

Blessed are those who trust in the LORD.

They are like _____.

Tell a partner why you chose to write what you did.

 Want to do more? Go to your Portfolio to continue this activity.

At Home

Talk about things you trust, like your parents' love for you. How does nature show us that God loves us?

42   **WITNESS**

Copyright © by William H. Sadlier, Inc. All rights reserved.

Who is Jesus Christ?

Jesus Christ is the only Son of God the Father. God the Father chose the Blessed Virgin Mary to be the Mother of Jesus.

Jesus is both God and man. Jesus is fully God. Jesus did things only God can do. Jesus is fully human. Jesus lived and died. He rose from the dead three days later. Now Jesus lives with his Father in heaven. Jesus came to lead us to new life forever, too!

Go to the digital portal for a prayer of meditation.

"God sent his only Son into the world so that we might have life through him."

1 John 4:9

Jesus is truly God and truly Man.

Two thousand years ago in the city of Bethlehem, a baby was born. That baby was Jesus. As the Son of God, the Second Person of the Trinity, Jesus is truly God. Yet, he was born of Mary, which means he was also truly a man. Jesus is truly God and truly Man.

God the Father chose the Blessed Virgin Mary to be Jesus' Mother. God chose her, but he also *asked* her. He let her choose. Mary loved God and wanted to do God's will. She said yes to God!

In what ways do I say yes to God?

Did You Know?

 There are many titles for Mary.

God the Holy Spirit came to Mary in a special way, and she conceived her baby. When Mary had her baby, she named him Jesus, just as the angel said.

Babies are born every day. You were a baby once, too! Jesus was unlike any other baby who was ever born or will be born. Jesus is God and is also a human being. Jesus is the Second Person of the Blessed Trinity. Jesus is God the Son.

God the Son, Jesus, came to live in the world with us as a human being. Mary is the Mother of God. When Mary said yes to the Angel Gabriel, the Son of God became man. The Church has a word for this mystery. The word is **Incarnation**.

Faith Word

Incarnation the truth that the Son of God became man

Jesus is the greatest gift.

Jesus is God's only Son who became one of us. Jesus is like us in all things except sin. At Mass, we say that we believe this. We say these words in the Creed. We pray that we believe Jesus is "God from God, Light from Light, true God from true God."

We also bow as we pray: "He came down from heaven, and by the Holy Spirit was incarnate of the Virgin Mary, and became man."

God gave us his Son, Jesus, to show us that he loves us and wants us to be with him forever.

Activity

What is a way that you can show that you are thankful for the gift of Jesus?

_____

_____

_____

_____

_____

Jesus died on the Cross for us.

When we see a cross, it reminds us of Jesus. Jesus suffered and died on the Cross. All who knew and loved him were saddened, upset, and afraid at first.

But the Death of Jesus was an act of love for all humanity! Jesus died for the sins of all people. He offered his life for us. And then he rose again so that we might have eternal life. The Cross is a sign of God's love for all people.

Activity

Create a word cloud on the cross with some of the things you know about Jesus.

The Risen Jesus returned to heaven.

Everything Jesus did and said showed God's love for us. Jesus lived and died out of love for his Father, the Holy Spirit, and us. The Father raised Jesus from the dead to show his love for Jesus and for us. God loves us forever.

The Father raised Jesus from the dead to show us that we, too, can live with him forever. After he rose to new life, the Risen Jesus returned to God the Father in heaven.

Jesus loved and obeyed his Father during his life on earth. Mary loved and obeyed God during her life, too. Now Mary lives in heaven. She shares in the Resurrection of Jesus. We believe that the Resurrection of Jesus and his returning to heaven shows that God wants this for us, too.

God wants us to love and obey him for as long as we live. God wants us to live with him forever in heaven, too!

Faith Word

Incarnation

 Show What You Know

Complete the sentences using words from the Word Bank.

gift   Incarnation   Cross   heaven   Mother

1. The _____ is the truth that the Son of God became man.

2. Mary is the _____ of God.

3. Jesus is the greatest _____ God gave us.

4. The Risen Jesus returned to God the Father in _____.

5. Jesus died on the _____ for us.

Partners in Faith

Saint Elizabeth

Mary went to see Saint Elizabeth before Jesus was born. Saint Elizabeth was happy. She knew Jesus was the Lord! Saint John the Baptist was her son.

 Learn more about the life of Saint Elizabeth.

Copyright © by William H. Sadlier, Inc. All rights reserved.

How can I share the gifts God has given me?

Mini-Task

God has given us many gifts.

Think about something special about you. It might be a talent that you have or a special skill. What are you good at? What do you enjoy doing?

We can share our gifts and talents with others.

What is your special gift?

Whom will you share it with?

When will you share it?

Where will you share it?

Why will you share it?

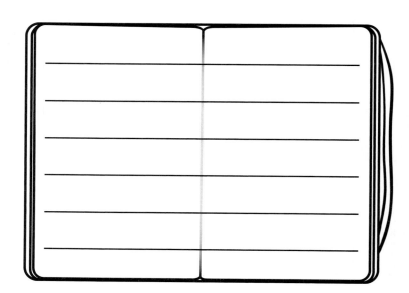

 Want to do more? Go to your Portfolio to continue this activity.

At

Jesus was once a baby. Share baby pictures of members of your family.

Copyright © by William H. Sadlier, Inc. All rights reserved.

What is the Church?

Jesus himself gave us the Church. The Apostles built the Church on what Jesus taught. The Church continues the work of Jesus. Jesus sent the Holy Spirit to guide the Church.

Today, the Church is led by the pope and bishops. All people who are baptized in the name of the Blessed Trinity, and are part of the Body of Christ, are part of the Church! We help the Church spread the word about Jesus.

Go to the digital portal for a prayer of intercession.

"In the Church, God is 'calling together' his people from all the ends of the earth."
Catechism of the Catholic Church, 751

The Church is the Body of Christ.

What do you think of when you hear the word *church*? Do you think of your church building where you and your family go to Mass? Many people do. There are many churches all over the world, but there is only one Church established by Jesus Christ.

The Church that Jesus gave us is much more than a building. The Church that Jesus gave us is the People of God.

The Church is also the **Body of Christ**. The Church has many members, just as a human body has many parts. All the parts work together. The People of God work together, too.

All the baptized are part of the Body of Christ. No two people in the Church are the same. Everyone has a different role or calling, because Jesus asks us to do different things. We serve God in different ways, and we are one Church! The Church is one Body of Christ.

What are some ways that I can use my gifts to serve God and help others?

Did You Know?

The Catholic Church speaks many languages.

Jesus sends the Holy Spirit to guide the Church.

Jesus knew his followers would feel lost without him. He promised to send the Holy Spirit to be with them. Jesus kept his promise. He sent God the Holy Spirit to be with his Church. The Holy Spirit helps the Church to grow and be holy.

Jesus wants us to come to know him more and more. The Holy Spirit guides the Church to help us believe in Jesus and to be holy. The Spirit guides the Church to help us to love God and one another as Jesus taught us to do.

Activity

A *church* is a building. The *Church* is a community.

Draw inside the church building some of the people you know who are part of the Church. Remember to draw yourself.

By the Holy Spirit, the Church continues Jesus' work.

Jesus invites everyone to be a part of his Church. But many people in the world have never heard of Jesus. Others do not know that God loves them and wants them to live with him forever.

God wants the whole world to know about him. That is why God the Father sent his Son, Jesus. Jesus is the Second Person of the Blessed Trinity. Jesus showed humankind who God is. The Holy Spirit is the Third Person of the Blessed Trinity, sent to help the Church continue Jesus' work.

The Church keeps spreading the word about Jesus. The Church, the People of God, is for everyone. This is such good news that the Church never stops sharing it.

We are the People of God. That means we are part of the Church. The work of the Church is our work, too. The Holy Spirit helps us to invite everyone into the Body of Christ. The Holy Spirit helps the Church to invite all people to believe in Jesus and be baptized.

Jesus built his Church on the Apostles.

The Church continues to do the work of Jesus today. Jesus chose Apostles to lead his Church after he returned to his Father in heaven. He chose Saint Peter to be the leader of the Apostles.

The Holy Spirit helped Saint Peter and the other Apostles to tell all people about Jesus. They helped the Church to grow.

"And so I say to you, you are Peter, and upon this rock I will build my church."

Matthew 16:18

Over the years, the Apostles chose new leaders to take their place. Today, the **pope** and the **bishops** do the Apostles' work. The pope is the leader of the Church who continues the work of Saint Peter. The bishops are leaders of the Church who carry on the work of the Apostles.

The pope and the bishops serve the whole Church. Priests and deacons also serve the Church. They lead us in prayer and show us that Jesus is with us.

We all help to do the work of the Church. God wants each of us to use the gifts he gave us to help spread his love to all people.

Faith Words

pope the leader of the Church who continues the work of Saint Peter

bishops leaders of the Church who carry on the work of the Apostles

Activity

Peter led the Church after Jesus went to heaven. Today, the pope, bishops, priests, and deacons are the ordained ministers who lead the Church. Many laypeople, such as catechists, altar servers, and musicians, support and help the ordained ministers who lead the Church. What are the names of the ordained ministers in your parish? What are the names of those who help them?

The pope's name is _____.

My bishop's name is _____.

My pastor's name is _____.

My catechist's name is _____.

Faith Words

Body of Christ   **pope**   **bishops**

 Show What You Know

Circle the correct answers.

1. The _____ is a way to describe the Church.

   Body of Christ | Person of Christ

2. The _____ is the leader of the Church.

   bishop | pope

3. Bishops carry on the work of the _____ .

   Apostles | Actions

Partners in Faith

Saint Paul

At first Saint Paul did not believe in Jesus. One day he saw Jesus in a vision. He spent the rest of his life talking about God. His letters are called epistles. They are part of the Bible.

 Learn more about the life of Saint Paul.

Copyright © by William H. Sadlier, Inc. All rights reserved.

Mini-Task

Placing a capital letter on a word can change its meaning.

The Body of Christ is the *Church*. The building we enter for Mass is a *church*.

Decide whether each clue in the chart means "Church" or "church." Put a check mark in the correct column. The first one is done for you.

	Church	church
Body of Christ	✔	
Where Mass is held		
Baptized people		
Has pews and kneelers		
Priests and deacons		

 Want to do more? Go to your Portfolio to continue this activity.

Think about all the people who go to your church. Name some people you see at Mass every Sunday.

Copyright © by William H. Sadlier, Inc. All rights reserved.

How do we celebrate what we believe?

The Lost Sheep

Unit Prayer

Leader: Saint Thérèse of Lisieux is known as the "Little Flower." She loved flowers. She saw herself as the little flower of Jesus. She gave glory to God by just being herself among all the other flowers in God's garden.

Listen to the stories of missionary disciples among us.

Let us pray:
Dear Jesus, we want to be "little flowers" by celebrating your love in our lives. When we are at Mass, we learn about this love in the readings. We know you are with us in Holy Communion. For all the gifts that you give us, we pray in thanksgiving.

Reader: For the beauty of the earth,

All: we thank you, Jesus.

Reader: For the celebration of the Mass,

All: we thank you, Jesus.

Reader: For the gift of flowers and gardens,

All: we thank you, Jesus.

Reader: With Saint Thérèse, we say: "My God, I love you!"

All: My God, I love you!

All sing: "Light of Christ"

 Unit Song: "Light of Christ," Tom Kendzia/OCP

Missionary Discipleship

How does the beauty of flowers and gardens make you know God's love? Have you ever given flowers to someone you love? Did you celebrate God's love in that gift? How did you feel?

How does God share his life with us?

The Church gathers to pray and worship God. Jesus gave us the sacraments to share God's life with us. The sacraments help us celebrate what we believe. They help our faith to grow stronger. The Blessed Trinity—God the Father, God the Son, and God the Holy Spirit—is with us in a special way through the sacraments. God shares his life and love with us through the sacraments.

Go to the digital portal for a prayer of petition.

"The sacraments strengthen faith and express it."
Catechism of the Catholic Church, 1133

Jesus Christ gave us the Church.

The Church is the Body of Christ. Jesus Christ is the Head of his Body, the Church. Christ and the Church are united and work together as one. The Church cannot do anything without Jesus!

Jesus is always with the Church. He is with us in the **liturgy**, the official public prayer of the Church. In the liturgy, the Church gives thanks and praise to God—the Father, Son, and Holy Spirit.

Jesus, the Head of the Church, and the other members of his Church work together as one. Jesus prays together with the members of his Body, the Church.

Faith Word

liturgy the official public prayer of the Church

What are some ways I open my heart to Jesus?

Did You Know?

When you pray, you participate in the prayer of the Church.

Jesus and the Holy Spirit share in the liturgy of the Church.

Jesus gave us the gift of the Church. The Blessed Trinity—God the Father, God the Son, and God the Holy Spirit—is present with the Church.

God the Holy Spirit makes the Church holy and guides her liturgy. The Holy Spirit builds up the work of the Church.

The Holy Spirit prepares us to meet Christ in the liturgy. The Holy Spirit helps us listen carefully to God's Word. We pay attention to everything that Jesus said and did. The Holy Spirit also helps prepare us to share in the work of Jesus in the world. When we pray, the Holy Spirit helps us to know what Jesus wants us to do.

The liturgy helps make us holy. It helps our faith grow strong. It helps us work together with Jesus wherever we are.

Activity

The liturgy is the official public prayer of the Church.

Write a prayer to thank God for the prayers the Church says in the liturgy.

Share your prayer with others.

Jesus gave the Church special signs of grace called sacraments.

God loves us very much. God loves us so much that he sent his Son, Jesus, to save us.

God the Father, God the Son, and God the Holy Spirit are one. God the Father sent his Son, Jesus, to share the love of the Blessed Trinity with all people.

Faith Word

sacraments
special signs given to us by Jesus through which God shares his life and love with us

Jesus gave us the gift of the Church. He gave the Church seven rites to unite us to the love of the Blessed Trinity. These seven rites are called **sacraments**. The sacraments share God's life and love with us.

The whole Church celebrates the sacraments. Each sacrament helps us to grow closer to God.

God's life and love in us is called **grace**. The word *grace* means "gift." Grace is God's gift to us. Grace makes us holy. Grace also helps us live a holy life. Jesus shares God's grace with us every time the Church celebrates the sacraments.

The sacraments make God's love for us present. Through sign, word, and action, they give us the grace of God. They show that Jesus is with us. Through the sacraments, God blesses us, chooses us, unites us, heals us, and forgives us. Jesus gave us seven sacraments so that we could share in God's grace. The sacraments help us have life forever with God.

Activity

When we love others we show God's life and love in what we say and do. Work with a partner to put a check mark next to ways we love others and an X next to ways we do not love others.

X ✔

☐ ☐ sharing with friends

☐ ☐ taking something that does not belong to us

☐ ☐ helping someone who is hurt

☐ ☐ not doing chores

☐ ☐ praying for family members

What is one more way you can show God's love?

 _____

Sacramentals are sacred signs of the Church.

Jesus gave us the sacraments as special signs of God's grace, which give us that grace. Other signs of God's grace are called **sacramentals**. Sacramentals do not give grace like the sacraments. Instead, they help us prepare to receive God's grace by reminding us of God's presence in our lives. Sacramentals are blessings, actions, and objects that help us respond to God's grace received in the sacraments. The Church also uses sacramentals to help us prepare for the sacraments.

Faith Word

sacramentals
blessings, actions, and objects that help us respond to God's grace received in the sacraments

There are many kinds of sacramentals.
Sacramentals include:

- the cross or crucifix you look at while you pray
- a religious medal
- a special blessing from a priest
- blessing yourself with holy water
- praying the Rosary or other special prayers of the Church
- ashes
- the Paschal candle and baptismal font.

Sacramentals help us open our hearts to God's grace. They help us remember that God loves us.

ЧАЧАЧА

Faith Words

liturgy   sacraments
grace   sacramentals

 Show What You Know

Circle the word that answers each question.

1. What are the special signs given to us by Jesus through which God shares his life and love with us?

grace | sacraments

2. What is the official public prayer of the Church?

liturgy | sacramentals

3. What are blessings, actions, and objects that help us respond to God's grace received in the sacraments?

sacramentals | liturgy

Partners in Faith

Saint Faustina Kowalska

Jesus appeared to Saint Faustina. He asked her to paint his picture. It shows him with red and white rays of mercy coming from his heart. The painting is called the *Divine Mercy*.

 Learn more about the life of Saint Faustina.

Copyright © by William H. Sadlier, Inc. All rights reserved.

How do I share God's life with others?

Mini-Task

An acrostic poem is one where you use each letter of a word to write the poem. The poem should help you remember what the word means. It can be used to teach others what the word means.

Write an acrostic poem using the word *grace*. Use the letters below to begin a phrase about grace.

G   God is good all the time.

R   _____

A   _____

C   _____

E   _____

 Want to do more? Go to your Portfolio to continue this activity.

At Home

On Sunday when your family goes to Mass, talk about Jesus. Think about what you will thank Jesus for during the liturgy.

Copyright © by William H. Sadlier, Inc. All rights reserved.

How do we praise and thank God?

The Church gives praise and thanks to God all year long. Jesus Christ is the Head of his Body, the Church. We celebrate that Jesus came to share God's life with us. We remember that Jesus died and rose for us. The most important way the Church praises God is through the Mass. The Church also praises God for the saints. Saints are people who show us how to follow Jesus.

Go to the digital portal for a prayer of adoration.

"Therefore, our God, we give you thanks and we praise the majesty of your name."
1 Chronicles 29:13

The Church celebrates Jesus through the liturgy.

We call Sunday the Lord's Day because Jesus rose from the dead on the first day of the week. The Church gathers for the liturgy on the Lord's Day.

The Eucharist is at the center of the Church's liturgy. The celebration of the Eucharist takes place in the **Mass**. The Mass is the Church's greatest celebration. It is our most important liturgy. Every Sunday, we gather for Mass to thank God the Father for sending his Son, Jesus, to save us. We remember that Jesus died and rose for us. We praise God and ask the Holy Spirit to guide us.

In what ways do I praise God?

Did You Know?

 The word *Mass* is from a Latin word that means "send."

Christ is present in the Mass in many ways: He is present in the people gathered, in the priest and the ministers, in the readings from Sacred Scripture, and, most especially, in the Eucharist, which is the Body and Blood, Soul and Divinity of Christ.

 "Blessed be the God and Father of our Lord Jesus Christ, who has blessed us in Christ."
Ephesians 1:3

The Church year celebrates Jesus' Paschal Mystery.

Every time we gather for Mass, we celebrate that Jesus suffered, died, rose from the dead, and returned to his Father in heaven. These events are called the **Paschal Mystery**.

The Church celebrates the Paschal Mystery all year. The Church year also celebrates special seasons.

During each season of the Church year, we remember something important about Jesus. We remember when Mary waited to give birth to Jesus at Christmas. We remember when Jesus was born. We remember the time that Jesus spent with his disciples. We remember when Jesus died, rose, and went to live with his Father in heaven at Easter.

The seasons of the Church year help us to learn more about Jesus and to grow in love for him.

Faith Word

Paschal Mystery
Christ's suffering, Death, Resurrection from the dead, and Ascension into heaven

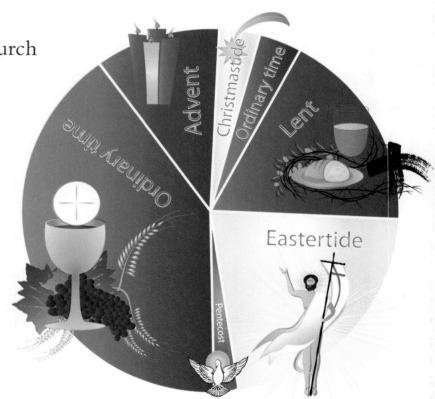

Activity

During the year, the Church celebrates important events in Jesus' life. Work in small groups to list some of these events. Share your group's list with the larger group.

We praise and thank God in many ways during the year.

When Jesus returned to his Father in heaven, he commissioned, or sent forth, the Apostles to continue his work. The Apostles told people about Jesus. They taught others what Jesus had taught them. They gathered people together to worship God the Father, God the Son, and God the Holy Spirit.

In the Mass, we pray as the Apostles taught us. The People of God are one Church. But we are also very different from each other!

God made us different, so our worship is different. All over the world, different people in different parishes sing different songs and pray in different languages. Even so, we are all one Church, praying as the Apostles did before us.

Blessings and devotions help us praise and thank God.

Faith Words

saints members of the Church who led holy lives and are happy with God forever in heaven

devotion a form of personal or communal prayer

blessing a sign of God's favor or a prayer asking God to make someone or something holy

The Church honors Mary, the Mother of God, and the **saints** on special days of the year. Saints are all the members of the Church who have led holy lives. Saints share with others their love for God in very special ways. After they die, they live happily with God forever in heaven.

We can show our honor of the saints by a **devotion**. A devotion is a form of personal or communal prayer. One special devotion is a prayer to Mary called the Rosary. We pray the Rosary using special beads. As we pray, we think about the lives of Jesus and Mary.

The saints ask God to give us his **blessings**. A blessing is a sign of God's favor. Blessing prayers ask God to make someone or something holy. We ask God to bless people, objects, and important events in our lives.

Activity

Write on the lines to complete the blessing prayer for someone you love or for something God has done for you. Teach your blessing prayer to a friend or to your family.

Dear God,

Thank you for _____. Everything you give us is good.

Please bless _____ and everyone. In Jesus' name, Amen.

Faith Words

Mass   Paschal Mystery   saints   devotion   blessing

 Show What You Know

Fill in each blank with the correct Faith Word.

1. The celebration of the Eucharist is the _____ .

2. A _____ is a form of personal or communal prayer.

3. Christ's suffering, Death, Resurrection from the dead, and Ascension into heaven is the _____ .

4. The _____ are all the members of the Church who have led holy lives and are happy with God forever in heaven.

5. A _____ is a sign of God's favor or a prayer asking God to make someone or something holy.

Partners in Faith

Saint John Vianney

Saint John Vianney was a French priest. He worked hard to bring people to God. He is the patron saint of parish priests.

 Learn more about the life of Saint John Vianney.

Copyright © by William H. Sadlier, Inc. All rights reserved.

Mini-Task

The Mass is the Church's greatest celebration. When we take part in the Sunday liturgy with our families, we are thanking God.

Design a poster that would encourage other families to join your family at Mass this Sunday. The poster should give information about the Mass and tell why it is important.

Sketch your poster here.

 Want to do more? Go to your Portfolio to continue this activity.

At Home

Share with your family memories of special seasons. What do you remember about Christmas? What do you celebrate at Easter?

Copyright © by William H. Sadlier, Inc. All rights reserved.

How do we become members of the Church?

Jesus gave us the sacraments so that we can share in God's life. Baptism makes us members of the Body of Christ. Confirmation increases the gifts of the Holy Spirit within us. The Eucharist unites us with Jesus and nourishes us. Together, these Sacraments of Christian Initiation make us members of the Church. They help us grow in our love for God.

Go to the digital portal for a prayer of blessing.

"Like living stones, let yourselves be built into a spiritual house."

1 Peter 2:5

The Sacraments of Christian Initiation make us members of the Church.

Jesus shares God's life with us in the Seven Sacraments of the Church. Three of these sacraments make us members of the Church. They are called the Sacraments of Christian Initiation. *Initiation* means "the beginning of something." The Sacraments of Baptism, Confirmation, and Eucharist begin and deepen our life in the Church.

In some parishes, people celebrate all three Sacraments of Christian Initiation at the same time. In other parishes, the people celebrate these sacraments at different times in their lives. Together, the Sacraments of Christian Initiation make us members of the Church. They help us to grow closer to God. They give us strength to follow Jesus as full members of the Body of Christ, the Church.

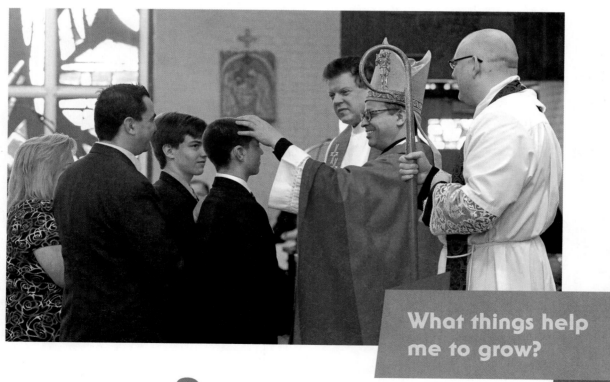

What things help me to grow?

Did You Know?

Godparents play a special role.

Baptism is new life in Jesus Christ.

Baptism is the first sacrament we receive. In this sacrament, we receive God's grace and become children of God and members of the Church. At your Baptism, your parish welcomed you as a new member of the Church. There are other effects of Baptism as well. Baptism washes away sin. It gives us new life in Christ.

Faith Word

Baptism the sacrament in which we receive God's sanctifying grace and become children of God and members of the Church

We receive the Sacrament of Baptism only once. Some people are baptized when they are babies. Others are baptized when they are older. Baptism marks you forever as a member of the Body of Christ.

By using water and the words "I baptize you in the name of the Father, and the Son, and the Holy Spirit," the priest (or deacon) celebrates the grace of new life given by Christ. This kind of grace is called sacramental grace. Water is a sign of the new life we receive at Baptism. We also call God's life and love in us grace. This kind of grace, actual grace, is the work God does in our daily lives to help us grow as his children. Actual and sanctifying graces help us follow Jesus. We need God's grace to live forever with him in heaven.

Activity

Design a welcome card for a newly baptized member of the Church. Include a message and pictures in your design.

Share your card design with a new member of your parish.

Confirmation seals us with the Gift of the Holy Spirit.

When we are baptized, each of us receives the Holy Spirit. **Confirmation** is the sacrament that seals us with the Gift of the Holy Spirit, who strengthens us to live out our baptismal promises. A seal is a spiritual sign. That seal makes the Gift of the Holy Spirit ours forever. This gift makes us stronger. After we are confirmed, the Holy Spirit gives us greater strength to follow Jesus.

Many people are confirmed as older children or young adults. A bishop is usually the one who confirms people. He extends his hands over each person and prays. The bishop dips his thumb in holy oil. He traces a cross on each person's forehead and says: "Be sealed with the Gift of the Holy Spirit" (Order of Confirmation, 27).

The anointing with oil shows that the Holy Spirit is with us. By the power of the Holy Spirit, this anointing claims us for Christ and calls us to share in his role as priest, prophet, and king.

Like Baptism, Confirmation marks us forever as members of the Body of Christ.

Faith Word

Confirmation the sacrament that seals us with the Gift of the Holy Spirit, who strengthens us to live our baptismal promises

The Eucharist unites us to Jesus and his sacrifice.

On the night before he died, Jesus shared a meal with his disciples. At the **Last Supper**, Jesus shared with his disciples his Body and Blood in the form of bread and wine. When we receive the Eucharist, we receive Jesus' Body and Blood.

At Mass, bread and wine become the Real Presence of the Body and Blood of Christ. This is done by the power of the Holy Spirit and through the words and actions of the priest. Only a priest can perform this action, called "consecration."

Faith Words

Last Supper the meal Jesus shared with his disciples on the night before he died, in which he gave us the Eucharist

Eucharist the sacrament in which we receive the Body and Blood of Jesus Christ

Holy Communion receiving the Body and Blood of Christ

The sacrament in which we receive the Body and Blood of Jesus Christ is called the **Eucharist**. The Eucharist is the Church's greatest sacrament. Receiving the Body and Blood of Christ in the Eucharist is called **Holy Communion**.

A gift offered to God is called a **sacrifice**. Jesus gave up his life as a sacrifice for us. When we celebrate the Eucharist, we remember that Jesus died and rose from the dead so that we might live with God forever.

Faith Word

sacrifice a gift offered to God

"Then he took the bread, said the blessing, broke it, and gave it to them, saying, 'This is my body, which will be given for you; do this in memory of me.'" Luke 22:19

Jesus made the greatest sacrifice of all time. Through the Holy Spirit and the ministry of the priest, Jesus is really present in the Eucharistic sacrifice. Holy Communion unites us to Jesus, to one another in the Body of Christ, and to the sacrifice he offered for us.

The Last Supper © 2018
John August Swanson/Eyekons

Activity

Think about a time when you gave up something as a gift to another person. What was it like to make this sacrifice? Tell a friend.

Faith Words

Baptism   Confirmation

Last Supper   Eucharist

Holy Communion   sacrifice

 Show What You Know

Match each term to the correct definition.

1. Last Supper — a gift offered to God

2. sacrifice — sacrament that seals us with the Gift of the Holy Spirit

3. Baptism — meal Jesus shared with his disciples the night before he died

4. Holy Communion — the sacrament of the Body and Blood of Jesus Christ

5. Eucharist — receiving the Body and Blood of Christ

6. Confirmation — the sacrament in which we receive God's grace and become children of God and members of the Church

Partners in Faith

Saint Catherine of Siena

Saint Catherine of Siena had many brothers and sisters. She lived at home and helped her family. She loved to receive the Eucharist. She knew it was the Body and Blood of Jesus.

 Learn more about the life of Saint Catherine of Siena.

Copyright © by William H. Sadlier, Inc. All rights reserved.

How can you show new life in Jesus Christ?

Mini-Task

The Sacraments of Christian Initiation are Baptism, Confirmation, and Eucharist. The three sacraments are alike, but they are also different. Review the lesson for information about each sacrament.

Now imagine that you are a reporter for a local TV news channel that also has a Web site. You are asked to write a story about the Sacraments of Christian Initiation that will inspire your viewers to learn more about the sacraments.

Write three major facts that will shape your news story.

_____

_____

_____

 Want to do more? Go to your Portfolio to continue this activity.

Invite your family members to talk about their Baptism or Confirmation. Ask them to share a time when celebrating the Eucharist has helped them and your family.

Copyright © by William H. Sadlier, Inc. All rights reserved.

How do we celebrate God's forgiveness and healing?

Jesus taught his followers about God's love and forgiveness. He healed those who were sick. He forgave people who were sorry for their sins. When he did this, he showed that God has power over sickness and sin. Today, the Church continues to celebrate God's forgiveness and healing in the Sacrament of Penance and Reconciliation.

Go to the digital portal for a *Lectio* and *Visio Divina* prayer.

"Hear us, Lord, for you are merciful and kind. . . . Make us living signs of your love."

Rite of Penance

God loves and forgives us.

The Bible has many stories that show how much God loves us. One of these stories is about a shepherd who loses one of his sheep.

God is like that shepherd. When we lose our way, God will look for us. He waits for us to say we are sorry.

God is always ready to forgive us. *To forgive* means "to accept someone's apology and continue to love them after they have hurt us." Forgiveness is a sign of God's love and mercy. When we forgive, we show God's love to others. God wants us to forgive and to let those who have hurt us try to make things better.

In what ways do I show God's love to others?

Did You Know?

Like a shepherd, God loves and cares for us.

We think about our words, thoughts, and behaviors.

Sin is any thought, word, or action that we freely choose to do even though we know that it offends God or our neighbor. Sins are different from mistakes or accidents. When we sin, we turn away from God.

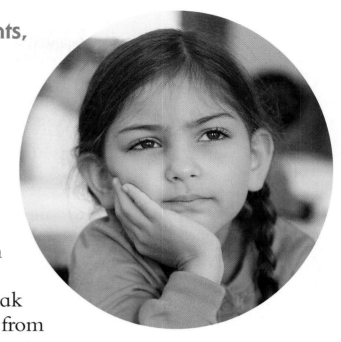

There are two kinds of sin. A venial sin hurts our friendship with God, but we still share in God's grace. When we break our friendship with God and turn away from him completely, we commit a mortal sin.

Activity

Think about your thoughts, words, and actions.

In the first bubble, write a thought, word, or action that shows love for God and others.

In the second bubble, write an action that is a mistake.

In the third bubble, write something that is a sin.

In the Sacrament of Penance and Reconciliation, we tell both mortal sins and venial sins and ask God's forgiveness. We can then receive God's forgiveness and healing. God has given each person a **conscience**. This gift helps a person to know what is right and what is wrong.

Faith Word

conscience God's gift that helps us to know right from wrong

Before we celebrate the Sacrament of Penance, we think about our sins. This is called an examination of conscience. When we make an examination of conscience, we think about our thoughts, words, and actions.

We say a prayer to show we are sorry for our sins. One way to do this is with an Act of Contrition.

 Act of Contrition

An Act of Contrition

My God,
I am sorry for my sins with all my heart.
In choosing to do wrong
and failing to do good,
I have sinned against you
whom I should love above all things.
I firmly intend, with your help,
to do penance, to sin no more,
and to avoid whatever leads me to sin.
Our Savior Jesus Christ
suffered and died for us.
In his name, my God, have mercy.

We celebrate God's forgiveness and healing in the Sacraments of Penance and Reconciliation and Anointing of the Sick.

The Sacrament of Penance and Reconciliation and the Sacrament of the Anointing of the Sick are called the Sacraments of Healing.

Through the Anointing of the Sick, a person receives the strength and courage to be at peace during a time of serious illness. People can make a **confession** when they are anointed. This is telling one's sins to the priest. Forgiveness can bring healing.

Through the Sacrament of Penance, we ask God's forgiveness. We make a confession. The priest cannot tell anyone the sins we confess.

After we confess our sins, the priest tells us to say a prayer or to do a kind act to repair the harm of our sins. This is called a **penance**.

The priest then asks us to express sorrow for our sins and promise not to sin again. This is **contrition**. *Contrition* is another word for *sorrow*.

We say an Act of Contrition to tell God we are sorry. We promise not to sin again. The priest acting in the name of God and the Church forgives our sins. This is called **absolution**.

Confession, penance, contrition, and absolution are always part of the Sacrament of Penance and Reconciliation.

Faith Words

confession telling our sins to the priest in the Sacrament of Penance

penance a prayer or kind act we do to repair the harm from our sins

contrition being sorry for our sins and promising not to sin again

absolution God's forgiveness of our sins, given by the priest in the Sacrament of Penance

God shows his mercy and love in the Sacrament of Penance.

When we celebrate the Sacrament of Penance, we receive God's forgiveness and peace. We are at peace with God and one another. We are forgiven for our sins.

Another word for God's love and forgiveness is **mercy**. God will always forgive us when we are sorry.

Faith Word

mercy God's love and forgiveness

"And when he does find it, he sets it on his shoulders with great joy and, upon his arrival home, he calls together his friends and neighbors and says to them, 'Rejoice with me because I have found my lost sheep.'" Luke 15:5–6

Activity

Color all the ♡ spaces green. Color all the ☆ spaces blue. Read what you see.

Faith Words

conscience	confession	penance
contrition	absolution	mercy

 Show What You Know

Fill in each blank with a Faith Word to complete the sentences.

1. Another word for *sorrow* is _____.

2. Forgiveness of sins by a priest acting in the name of God and

   the Church is _____.

3. Telling our sins to the priest is called _____.

4. A kind act or prayer to make up for our sins is called

   _____.

5. Our _____ helps us know
   right from wrong.

Partners in Faith

Saint Teresa of Calcutta

Saint Teresa of Calcutta took care of people who had no one to care for them. She asked people to forgive others who had hurt them.

 Learn more about the life of Saint Teresa of Calcutta.

Copyright © by William H. Sadlier, Inc. All rights reserved.

How can I help others know God's forgiveness and healing?

Mini-Task

A public service announcement (PSA) is a message that is shared on TV, radio, or other media. A PSA tells people about something important or helps them make a change.

What message do you want to share about God's forgiveness and healing?

_____

_____

_____

Write your idea or use a picture to start creating your message.

_____

_____

_____

Want to do more? Go to your Portfolio to continue this activity.

At Home

Name a few ways that you, as a family, share God's forgiveness and healing. How can you remind one another about God's forgiveness and healing?

Copyright © by William H. Sadlier, Inc. All rights reserved.

God gives each one of us many gifts. He wants us to share those gifts with others. God calls us to serve him by serving the Church and one another. God calls some people to serve him through Marriage or Holy Orders. Marriage and Holy Orders are sacraments. They are called Sacraments at the Service of Communion.

Go to the digital portal for a prayer of thanksgiving.

"There are different forms of service but the same Lord."
1 Corinthians 12:5

We are called to serve Christ and the Church in special ways.

Each one of us is called by God for a purpose. God invites us to love and serve him. God wants us all to share in the work of Jesus. We can pray with our parish. We can love and care for our families. We can help people who are in need.

As we grow older, we are called to serve God. God calls some people to marriage and family life. Some men are called to be ordained. God calls some people to a consecrated life as laypeople or religious sisters or brothers. To be consecrated means that one's life is dedicated in a special way to God and the Church. These are all important ways to serve God and share his love with others.

God has a job for each one of us! He wants us to work together to make the Church strong and holy.

What are some ways that I love and serve God?

Did You Know?

There are many forms of service.

God calls and gifts certain people to guide the Church.

All members of the Church share the work of Christ. Some members are called to serve in special ways.

Holy Orders is the sacrament through which a baptized man becomes a bishop, priest, or deacon. The pope chooses some priests to become bishops. Bishops carry on the work of the Apostles in proclaiming the Gospel message in three important ways: teaching, governing, and sanctifying. Priests and deacons share in these tasks, but in different degrees. Priests lead and serve the parish. They celebrate Mass and all the sacraments. Deacons assist at Mass and may celebrate Baptisms and marriages.

Faith Word

Holy Orders the sacrament through which a baptized man becomes a bishop, priest, or deacon

Activity

Priests help us to know more about God. With a small group, write some of the ways your parish priest helps you to know God. Share your notes with the larger group.

> "Keep watch over yourselves and over the whole flock of which the holy Spirit has appointed you overseers, in which you tend the church of God."
>
> Acts of the Apostles 20:28

Bishops, priests, and deacons promise to spend their lives serving God and the Church. They lead and guide the Church and pass on Jesus' teachings.

Bishops, priests, and deacons are ordained through the Sacrament of Holy Orders. This means they have been set apart by God. God chooses these men to share his love with people like Jesus did. Like priests, deacons are ordained. They are ordained to a ministry of service. They serve the priests, bishops, and the people.

Marriage is a special way to show God's love.

Many men and women are called to serve God as married people. **Matrimony** is another word for *marriage*. In Matrimony, a baptized man and baptized woman promise to serve God and the Church together in the Sacrament of Matrimony. They become husband and wife. Married people promise to love and be faithful to each other for the rest of their lives.

Married people love each other the way Christ loves his Church. They share God's love in special ways with each other and with their children.

Mothers and fathers are usually the first people to teach their children about Jesus and the Church. They show their children how to live as disciples. They share God's love with their families.

Faith Word

Matrimony the sacrament in which a baptized man and baptized woman become husband and wife

"As for me and my household, we will serve the Lord."

Joshua 24:15

We learn to pray in our family.

Jesus is both fully human and fully divine. Mary and Joseph taught him how to pray as they did. He grew in knowledge of Jewish prayers and rituals. Yet, as the divine Son of God, Jesus already knew how to speak to God the Father from his heart.

When we pray, we speak to God and listen to God. Prayer helps us grow closer to God. We can learn to pray in our family.

One of the most important ways for a family to pray together is at Mass every Sunday. You might also pray before meals, before bed, or at other times. God always hears our prayers! Thank God for his blessings, and ask him to be with you.

Activity

One way to learn to pray is by using your fingers.

On your first finger, tell God you **adore** him.

On your second finger, **confess** something you did wrong.

On your next finger, **thank** God for his love.

On your baby finger, **say** something you need God to help you with.

On your thumb, say "**Amen!**"

Faith Words

Holy Orders   Matrimony

 Show What You Know

Unscramble the words to answer the questions.

yoHl Osdrre   Mtiarmnoy

What is the sacrament through which a baptized man becomes a bishop, priest, or deacon?

_____

What is the sacrament in which a baptized man and baptized woman become husband and wife?

_____

Partners in Faith

Blessed Luigi and Maria Beltrame

Blessed Luigi and Maria Beltrame were married. Luigi was a lawyer. Maria was a professor. They had four children and loved their family. They were the first couple to be named "Blessed" at the same time.

 Learn more about the life of Blessed Luigi and Maria Beltrame.

Copyright © by William H. Sadlier, Inc. All rights reserved.

What gifts can I give the Church?

Mini-Task

Do you know someone who has been called by God to serve the Church and others?

Who is this person? What are his or her gifts?

Write a thank-you letter to someone who has been called by God to serve.

In your letter:

- write the proper name of the person you are writing

- name a gift the person is sharing with the Church

- use words of thanks

- sign your name

Date: _____

Dear _____,

In Jesus' name,

_____

 Want to do more? Go to your Portfolio to continue this activity.

 **At Home**

In the morning, with your family, try to take a minute to say thank you to God. Pray that the people in your family stay close to Jesus all day.

Copyright © by William H. Sadlier, Inc. All rights reserved.

How do we live what we believe?

Unit 3
The Faith Lived

The Road to Damascus

Unit Prayer

Leader: Saint Thérèse of Lisieux felt that God wanted her to "be love" in the world. Jesus taught us how to live a life of love to everyone we meet. Let us listen now to how we can "be love" in the world.

Listen to the stories of missionary disciples among us.

O God, you sent us your Son, Jesus, who taught us how to love each other. Help us to be love in the world.

All: Dear Jesus, help us to be love.

Leader: Lord Jesus, you taught us to love one another as you have loved us.

All: Dear Jesus, help us to be love.

Leader: Lord Jesus, you showed us how much you love us by dying on the Cross.

All: Dear Jesus, help us to be love.

Leader: On Easter, you rose from the dead, and your Holy Spirit lives in us to show us how to be love.

All: Dear Jesus, help us to be love.

All sing: "Prayer of St. Francis"

 Unit Song: "Prayer of St. Francis," Sebastian Temple/OCP

Missionary Discipleship

When have your parents or guardians shown you how they love you? What did you do? When have you shown someone how much you love him or her? When have you seen how much God loves you?

How do we know God loves us?

Human beings are God's most special creatures. God made us in his own image. God wants us to love and care for each other as he does. Jesus shows us how to love God, ourselves, and others. God also gives us rules. God's rules help us to know what he wants and to make good choices.

Go to the digital portal for a prayer of thanksgiving.

"And whatever you do, in word or in deed, do everything in the name of the Lord Jesus."

Colossians 3:17

Humans are God's most special creatures.

The Bible tells us that God made us in his own image and likeness. What does that mean? We are reflections of God himself and made to be like him.

> "The love of God has been poured out into our hearts through the holy Spirit that has been given to us."
>
> Romans 5:5

Human beings are God's most special creatures. God gave us gifts that he gave no other creature. We seek to do good because God is good. We love because God loves. God is love. We have faith so that we can know God and trust in him.

God also showed us how special we are by giving us Jesus. Jesus is God, the Son, who became man, like us in all things except sin. Jesus came to show us that we have a special place in creation. He came to show us that God wants us to live with him forever in heaven.

What are some ways that I am special?

Did You Know?

Every child is important in God's eyes.

We are all important and equal in God's eyes.

Every person God created is loved and treasured by him. God created all people to be equal, important, and good.

Every human life is **sacred**, or holy. God calls on all people to be holy as he is holy. We are holy when we love one another and keep God's Commandments.

Faith Word

sacred holy

Jesus taught that God is our Father. We are all God's children. God loves each one of us.

How does God want his children to treat each other? He wants us to love each other and to take care of each other. Everything we say and do should show people that God loves each one of his children. Jesus showed us how to do this by the way he treated others.

Activity

Circle the ways we can show our love for God.
Mark an X through the ways that do not show God's love.

Help a friend | Visit a grandparent | Be polite

Not play with someone | Share a treat | Tell a lie

Say a prayer | Obey parents

What can you do this week to show God's love? Tell a friend.

Jesus teaches us how to love God.

Jesus loved everyone. He helped people and spent time with them. He welcomed them when others did not.

God wants us to love as Jesus did, but God lets us choose for ourselves. God's gift of the freedom and ability to choose what to do is called **free will**. Sometimes we choose what is loving and good. Sometimes we do not.

Faith Word

free will God's gift of the freedom and ability to choose what to do

If you tip over one domino in a row of dominoes, the domino falls down. The other dominoes in the row fall down, too. Our choices are sometimes like that. A good choice can make something good happen. A bad choice can make something bad happen. Every choice that we make might help or hurt someone. Every choice can turn us toward God or away from God.

If we want to live as Jesus taught, we take time to think before we act. We ask ourselves: "Is this what God wants me to do? Does this show love for God, myself, and others?"

God wants us to choose what is loving and good. God wants us to act like the holy people he made us to be.

Jesus shows us that God's laws are built on love.

God cares about what happens to all of his children. He wants us to treat each other with love and respect.

God gives us laws to protect everyone. God's laws are called commandments. The commandments help us do what God wants. They help us treat each other as God's children.

Before Jesus came, God's people followed many rules about everyday life. They had rules for how to eat and what to wear. When Jesus came, he said the most important law for us to follow was to love God above all things and our neighbor as ourselves. This is called the **Great Commandment.** When we obey the Great Commandment, we are living as God made us to live.

Activity

Imagine that there is a new person in your group. Talk with a partner about how you could include the new person when you play. Role-play a brief scene to show the group how you could love the new person as Jesus does.

The Great Commandment shows us that all of God's laws are built on love.

"You shall love the Lord, your God, with all your heart, with all your being, with all your strength, and with all your mind, and your neighbor as yourself."

Luke 10:27

Jesus taught us to follow his example. He taught us to share God's love with everyone. The commandments help us to love as Jesus taught us. When we follow God's laws, we choose to do what God wants and to be like him.

Faith Words

sacred   free will

Great Commandment

 Show What You Know

Match the terms to the correct definitions.

1. free will

2. Great Commandment

3. sacred

Jesus' teaching to love God, ourselves, and others

holy

God's gift of the freedom and ability to choose what to do

Partners in Faith

Saint Benedict Joseph Labre

As a young man, Saint Benedict was homeless. He traveled around Europe, going to churches and praying. Saint Benedict cared for and prayed for other homeless people he met. He shared his food and clothing. He had a special love for Mary and Jesus. He is the patron saint of the homeless.

 Learn more about the life of Saint Benedict Joseph Labre.

Copyright © by William H. Sadlier, Inc. All rights reserved.

How do I show my love for God?

Mini-Task

Jesus taught us to follow his example. He taught us to share God's love with everyone. We show our love for God by respecting and caring for others.

Design a logo for a T-shirt that would remind people that everyone is holy.

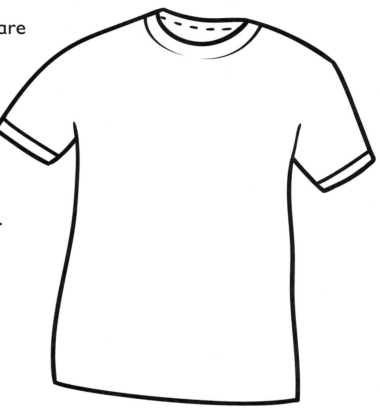

 **Want to do more? Go to your Portfolio to continue this activity.**

At Home

Go outside with your family. Look at the different parts of God's creation: the sky, the plants, the animals—and all the members of your family. Together, thank God for creating the world.

Copyright © by William H. Sadlier, Inc. All rights reserved.

How do we respond to God's love?

God wants us to be happy with him forever. To be happy, we must do what is right. God gave us a conscience to help us. Jesus gave us the Beatitudes to show us how to live in peace with one another. Virtues like faith, hope, and charity help us to trust and love God. Virtues help us to treat all people with fairness and respect.

Go to the digital portal for a prayer of blessing.

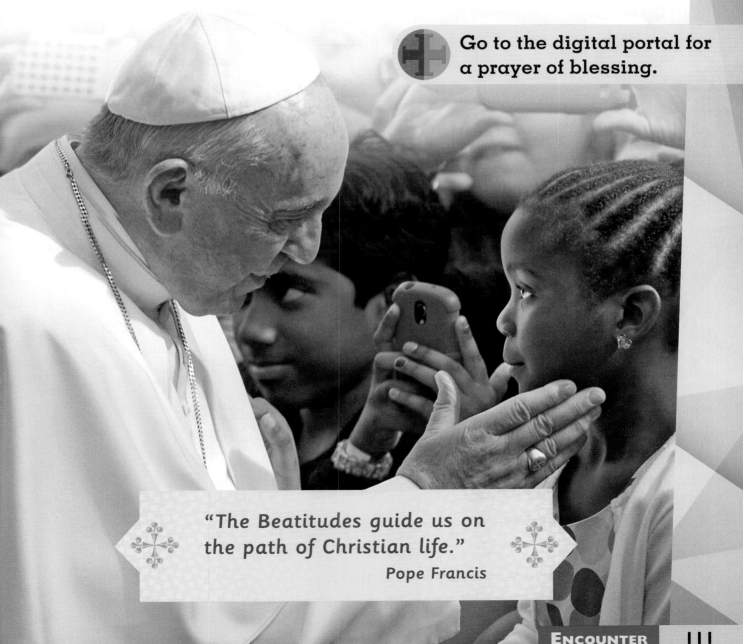

"The Beatitudes guide us on the path of Christian life."

Pope Francis

Jesus teaches us how to be happy.

Jesus taught that we can be happy forever in heaven if we live as his followers. The **Beatitudes** are teachings of Jesus that describe how to live as his followers. The Beatitudes teach that we should be humble and forgiving. We should work for peace and treat others fairly. We should stand up for what is right, even when it is hard. These are all ways to love God and our neighbor.

Jesus gave us the Beatitudes to show us how to live. Following the Beatitudes will give us happiness that lasts forever. If we follow Jesus' example and try to do what is right and good, we can be happy with God forever in heaven.

Faith Word

Beatitudes teachings of Jesus that describe the way to live as his followers

When do I stand up for what is right?

Did You Know?

 Helping others makes you happy.

Our conscience helps us know right from wrong.

It can be hard to live as God wants us to. Our **conscience** helps us. Our conscience is a gift from God that helps us to know right from wrong. It is God speaking in our hearts.

Faith Word

conscience God's gift that helps us to know right from wrong

God wants us to form a good conscience and listen to it. He also wants us to learn about his laws from the Bible and from the Church. Learning about God's laws helps us to form a good conscience and make good choices. When we learn about what God wants for us, we are better able to choose to do good and avoid what is bad. We also need to pray for the grace to do good.

God places his laws in our hearts. Learning about God's laws and also listening to our hearts help us to choose what God wants for us.

Activity

Beatitude means "blessed." When we do what Jesus asks, we bless others and ourselves. How is the child in the picture following Jesus' teaching?

_____

Virtues are habits of doing good.

As followers of Jesus, we try to make good choices every day. We also try to build good habits. Good habits help us choose what is right more often. A **virtue** is a good habit that helps us act as God wants us to. God gives us grace to do this. Grace makes it easier for us to keep up these good habits.

Faith Word

virtue a good habit that helps us act as God wants us to

Three important virtues God gives us are faith, hope, and charity. *Charity* is another word for *love*. We have faith in God and believe in him. We hope to live forever with God in heaven. We love as Jesus taught us. Faith, hope, and charity help us do what is right and good. The more we practice these virtues, the stronger they become.

The Holy Spirit also helps baptized and confirmed people live as followers of Jesus. The Holy Spirit gives us grace to do what is right, even when it is hard. With the help of the Holy Spirit, we can be fair and humble. We can treat others with respect and stand up for what we believe.

When we trust in God to help us do what is right, we know we can be happy.

 "Happy the one who trusts in the LORD!"

Proverbs 16:20

Jesus teaches us to treat all people fairly.

The grace of Christ helps us keep God's laws. When we sin, grace moves us to want to confess our sin and receive God's forgiveness.

We honor and obey God when we work together for peace and **justice**. *Justice* means "fair and respectful treatment of others." All people deserve respect because they were made by God in his own image and are loved by him.

Faith Word

justice fair and respectful treatment of others

Jesus taught us to treat all people fairly. We must work together to make sure the world is just. This means that we care for each other and stand up for each other. We make sure our laws are fair for everyone, not just for some people. We make sure all people have what they need.

When we work for peace and justice, it helps the whole human family.

Activity

Justice means "fair and respectful treatment of others."
List three ways you play fair.

1. _____

2. _____

3. _____

Tell a friend how you feel when you are not treated fairly.

Faith Words

Beatitudes   conscience

virtue   justice

 Show What You Know

In your own words, write definitions for the terms.

virtue _____

_____

justice _____

_____

Beatitudes _____

_____

conscience _____

Partners in Faith

Saint John Chrysostom

Saint John Chrysostom lived in what is now Turkey. He explained what Jesus said to many people. He is a famous teacher in the Church. He told people to take care of the poor.

 Learn more about the life of Saint John Chrysostom.

Copyright © by William H. Sadlier, Inc. All rights reserved.

Mini-Task

In this lesson, you learned more about Jesus.

Jesus shows us how to treat people with kindness. Write three acts of kindness that you can share with others. Choose one and plan to do it this week.

_____

_____

_____

_____

_____

_____

 Want to do more? Go to your Portfolio to continue this activity.

God speaks to us in the quiet of our hearts. But we cannot hear him unless we are quiet. Sit quietly with your family, and have each member hold a rosary or hold hands to remind each other of God's love.

Copyright © by William H. Sadlier, Inc. All rights reserved.

How does God teach us to love?

The commandments tell us how God expects us to live. Jesus taught us how to follow God's laws. The Church reminds us of Jesus' teachings and encourages us to follow his example. When we follow the commandments, we honor and respect God. We treat our families and other people with love and respect. We build up Christ's Church. God's laws help us to live in the truth.

Go to the digital portal for a prayer of adoration.

"Take to heart my commands;
For many days, and years of life,
and peace, will they bring you."
Proverbs 3:1–2

God's laws build up Christ's Church.

God wants us to show our love for him. He gave us special laws to help us, called the **Ten Commandments.**

Faith Word

Ten Commandments ten special laws God gave to his people

 Ten Commandments

The Ten Commandments show us how God wants us to live. They were written in the Bible before Jesus was born. We have read in the Bible how these laws helped prepare God's people to follow the Great Commandment that Jesus taught.

By following the Ten Commandments, we know how to love God and our neighbor.

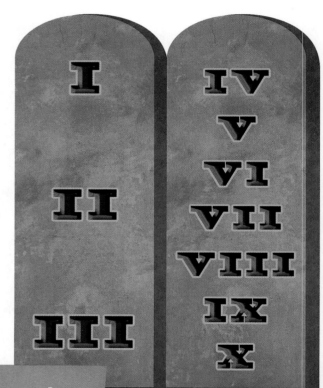

Jesus said: "You are my friends if you do what I command you" (John 15:14). We are disciples of Jesus when we keep the commandments. By keeping the commandments, we grow in holiness together. This builds up the Church that Jesus gave us, and it helps to make the Church holy. When we disobey God's laws, this hurts the Body of Christ.

What rules make me strong?

Did You Know?

 A commandment is more than a law.

God's commandments show us how to love him.

The first three of the Ten Commandments show us how to love God.

1. **I am the Lord your God: you shall not have strange gods before me.** This means we believe in only one God. We trust in him more than anyone or anything.

2. **You shall not take the name of the Lord your God in vain.** This means we speak God's name only with love and respect.

3. **Remember to keep holy the Lord's Day.** This means we worship God and make the Lord's Day special. We go to Mass every Sunday. We make Sunday special by resting, spending time with people we love, and saying "thank you" for God's gifts.

When we obey these commandments, we show we love God above all things.

Activity

Read the Ten Commandments in your text. Choose one commandment. How can you keep this commandment this week? Write or draw a picture.

Share your picture or your writing with a friend.
Did you choose the same commandment?

The commandments show us how to love our families.

The other commandments show us how to love others. We start learning about the commandments and following them in our own homes by loving our families. Obeying God's laws at home means that we treat our parents and families with love and respect.

4. We respect and obey our parents.

5. We respect all human life.

6. We respect the sanctity of marriage.

7. We do not take anything that is not ours.

8. We tell the truth.

9. We show that we are thankful for the people we have been given.

10. We are thankful for what we own and do not get jealous of what others own.

Our families are where we first learn to follow Jesus. When we obey these commandments at home, we know that we are doing what Jesus asks us to do.

The Church teaches and guides us.

God gave us the community of the Church to help us live as he created us. The Church has laws that we follow. There are laws to help us to know and fulfill our responsibilities as members of the Church, called the **Precepts of the Church**. The Precepts of the Church remind us to receive the sacraments. The sacraments nourish and strengthen us to be disciples. There are five Precepts of the Church.

Faith Word

Precepts of the Church laws to help us to know and fulfill our responsibilities as members of the Church

The Precepts of the Church

• Attend Mass on Sundays and special holy days.

• Confess your sins at least once a year in the Sacrament of Penance and Reconciliation.

• Receive the Eucharist at least once a year during the Easter season.

• Obey the Church's rules about fasting, such as not eating meat on Fridays during Lent.

• Support the Church as well as you are able.

The pope, bishops, and all Church leaders, along with the entire Church, are to obey the commandments and the Precepts of the Church. The Holy Spirit guides them as they teach us and lead us to live as disciples of Christ. Our Church leaders help us follow Jesus by obeying all God's laws.

Activity

Look at the Precepts of the Church on page 123 in your book. Make a poster about one of the precepts. Write some of your ideas for your poster here.

Which precept did you choose?

_____

_____

_____

What can you show on your poster to tell about this precept?

_____

_____

_____

_____

Share your poster with your group.

Faith Words

Ten Commandments

Precepts of the Church

 Show What You Knowww

Circle the correct term to complete the sentence.

1. The _____ are laws to help us to know and fulfill our responsibilities as members of the Church.

   previews of the Church | Precepts of the Church

2. The _____ Commandment says we should obey our parents.
   First | Fourth

3. The _____ are special laws that God gave to his people.
   Ten Rules | Ten Commandments

4. God wants us to keep the Lord's _____ holy.
   Day | Diary

Partners in Faith

Saint Pius X

Saint Pius X wanted us to receive Jesus in the Eucharist as often as possible. He changed the age of First Communion from age 12 to age 7. We can receive the Eucharist at every Mass if we are in a state of grace.

 Learn more about the life of Saint Pius X.

Copyright © by William H. Sadlier, Inc. All rights reserved.

Mini-Task

Look at the photograph.

Think about which of God's laws this family is following.

How does this law show us God's love?

Turn and talk to a partner about the photograph.

 Want to do more? Go to your Portfolio to continue this activity.

What are your favorite games to play, inside or outside? As a family, talk about the rules of the games. How do the rules help make the games fun and fair to everyone?

Copyright © by William H. Sadlier, Inc. All rights reserved.

What turns us away from God's love?

All human beings sin. This means we choose to do things that we know are wrong. When we sin, we fail to love as Jesus taught us. Some sins are so serious that they break our friendship with God. Even small sins can become a bad habit. All sins go against God's plan for us. Yet God never stops loving us. He forgives us when we are sorry for our sins.

 Go to the digital portal for a prayer of petition.

"So for one who knows the right thing to do and does not do it, it is a sin."

James 4:17

Adam and Eve's disobedience means that all humans will sin.

The Bible tells a story about Adam and Eve, the first people God created.

Faith Word

Original Sin the first sin, which happened when the first man and woman, Adam and Eve, disobeyed God

"The Lord God gave the man this order: You are free to eat from any of the trees of the garden except the tree of knowledge of good and evil. From that tree you shall not eat."

Genesis 2:16–17

Adam and Eve did what God told them not to do. They turned away from the goodness of God.

That first sin is called **Original Sin**. It is like an inclination that was passed down to all people. Each one of us is born with that inclination. This means we all tend to sin.

Original Sin went against God's plan for us. When we were baptized, we were freed from sin and we shared in God's goodness again.

How do I feel when I lose something that is special?

Did You Know?

We have many choices in life.

Sin keeps us from loving each other as we should.

In the Great Commandment, Jesus taught us to love God and our neighbor. Sin is any thought, word, or deed that keeps us from loving as Jesus taught. We sin any time we disobey God's laws. We sin when we choose not to love as Jesus did.

We are responsible for whatever happens when we choose to sin. When we sin, we offend God and harm ourselves. When we sin, we may harm other people.

Sometimes we might do harm by mistake. This is not a sin. Our sins are only those things that we choose to do even though we know they are wrong.

Activity

Baptism gives us strength and courage through the Holy Spirit. Ask three friends how they might avoid

- cheating when you see the answers to a test

- ignoring someone who is teasing a friend

- telling a lie when you get in trouble.

Talk about ways you can use your strength and courage to make the right choices.

Sin hurts our friendship with God.

God lets us choose whether or not we will follow his commandments and love as Jesus taught. Even though we have a choice, sin goes against God's plan for us. Sin keeps us from being the people God made us to be.

When we sin, we hurt our friendship with God. Sins turn us away from God's love. The good news is that God never turns away from us. God never stops loving us. He will always forgive us when we say we are sorry and try to do better.

In the Sacrament of Penance and Reconciliation, we turn back to God. We confess our sins and promise to do better. We show that we want to follow Jesus and live as God's children again.

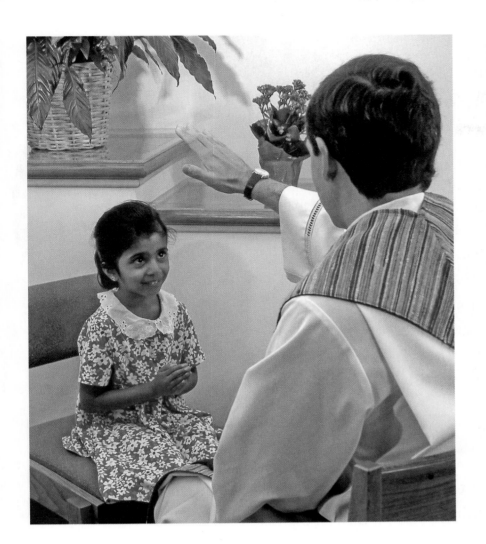

mortal sins sins that break our friendship with God

venial sins sins that hurt our friendship with God

vices bad habits that hurt our friendship with God and with one another

Less serious sins can lead to serious ones.

Some sins are so serious that they turn us away from God. **Mortal sins** break our relationship with God. People who commit a mortal sin do not share in God's life and help. We must tell these sins to a priest in the Sacrament of Penance and Reconciliation to receive God's forgiveness.

Other sins are less serious. **Venial sins** hurt our relationship with God. Yet people who commit venial sins still share in God's grace.

Even if a sin is not serious, it can *become* serious if we commit it over and over. When we choose to sin again and again, our sins may become **vices**. Vices are bad habits that hurt our friendship with God and with one another.

Bad habits may lead us to

- think we are better than others
- take more than our share of God's gifts
- be jealous of the gifts of others
- wish harm to others
- forget about God's love
- miss Mass on Sunday.

The Holy Spirit can give us grace to fight against vices. Grace strengthens us to resist temptation to sin and build loving habits instead.

Activity

It is important to know that mistakes are not sins. You sin when you know something is wrong and you do it anyway.

With a partner, use the chart to decide whether something is a sin or not a sin. Circle Yes or No for each.

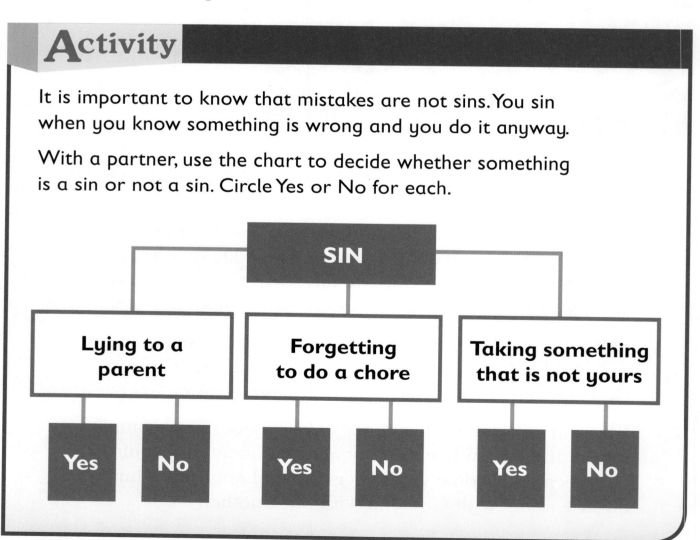

SIN

Lying to a parent	Forgetting to do a chore	Taking something that is not yours
Yes No	Yes No	Yes No

Faith Words

Original Sin   **mortal sins**

venial sins   **vices**

 Show What You Know

Fill in the blanks to complete the sentences.

1. Sins that break our friendship with God are _____ sins.

2. _____ are bad habits that hurt our friendship with God and with one another.

3. Sins that hurt our friendship with God are _____ sins.

4. _____ Sin happened when the first man and woman disobeyed God.

Partners in Faith

Saint Isidore of Seville

Saint Isidore wanted to know everything he could about the world. Yet he believed that confession and friendship with God are the most important things. He is the patron saint of the Internet.

 Learn more about the life of Saint Isidore of Seville.

Copyright © by William H. Sadlier, Inc. All rights reserved.

How can I be who God made me to be?

Mini-Task

Draw a comic strip about a superhero who helps someone change his or her bad habits to doing good.

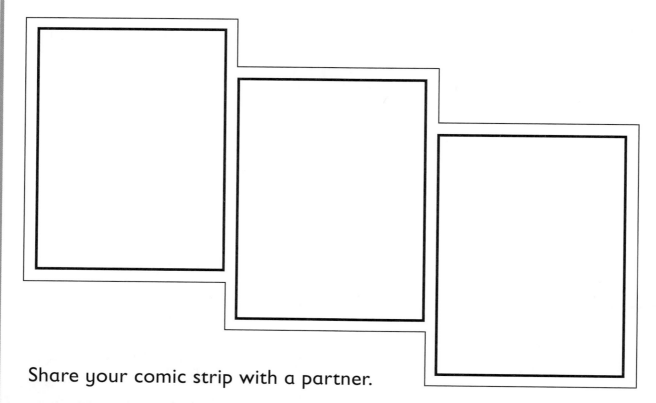

Share your comic strip with a partner.

 Want to do more? Go to your Portfolio to continue this activity.

At Home

Talk with your family about the difference between making a mistake and doing something hurtful on purpose.

Copyright © by William H. Sadlier, Inc. All rights reserved.

What turns us toward God's love?

Jesus lived, died, and rose from the dead to free us from sin so we could live forever with God. Baptism unites us with Christ and allows us to share in God's grace. Grace is a gift that helps us turn away from sin. If we accept God's grace, our hearts can be healed from sin and made holy.

Go to the digital portal for a *Lectio* and *Visio Divina* prayer.

"I have greatly sinned,
in my thoughts and in my words,
in what I have done and in what I have
failed to do."

Penitential Act, *Roman Missal*

Through Jesus, we share in God's life and love.

Before Paul became one of Jesus' disciples, he did not believe in Jesus. He did everything he could to stop Jesus' disciples from spreading the Word of God.

When the Risen Jesus appeared to him, Paul was stunned. He changed and became a follower of Jesus.

Paul knew he had been a great sinner. Yet Paul chose a new life because of the grace of Jesus Christ. Paul spent the rest of his life teaching others about Jesus. He spread the word about Jesus far and wide. Paul blessed and strengthened members of the early Church by sharing the Good News of Jesus. Everything that Paul did was possible because of God's grace.

Through Jesus, each one of us shares in God's life and love. Just as Jesus invited Paul to love and follow him, God invites us. God gives us his grace to help us.

What can God help me to do?

Did You Know?

 People can change.

Grace helps us to live as God's children.

God calls each of us to live in his love and follow his commandments. God gives us grace to help us. There is nothing we can do to earn God's grace. He gives it to us freely because he loves us.

Through Baptism, we come to share in God's grace. Only Jesus is the divine Son of God, but Baptism makes us the "adopted" sons and daughters of God. In Baptism, we come to share in the life, Death, and Resurrection of Jesus Christ. Receiving the Eucharist and the other sacraments makes God's grace grow stronger in us.

> "Indeed, the grace of our Lord has been abundant, along with the faith and love that are in Christ Jesus."
>
> 1 Timothy 1:14

Activity

Write a line for a group poem about God's love. Use the words below for ideas.

creation   **love**   **goodness**   **Jesus**   **gift**   **grace**

_____

_____

When your whole group is finished, read aloud your poem together.

God wants to share his love with all of us. He gives us grace to help us live as his children.

It is because of God's grace that we can have life forever in heaven. Jesus said: "For human beings this is impossible, but for God all things are possible" (Matthew 19:26). Anything that God wants for us, he makes possible by his grace.

Grace helps us to grow in holiness.

Jesus is like a light shining in the darkness. He shows us the way to God. The grace of Christ helps us turn away from sin and turn toward the light instead. Jesus said: "I am the light of the world. Whoever follows me will not walk in darkness, but will have the light of life" (John 8:12).

God gives us grace because he loves us. If we open our hearts to the grace of Christ, it can heal us from sin. Grace heals our friendship with God and makes us holy.

Activity

Find a small object in the room. Keep it hidden behind your back. Ask a partner to try to guess what it is. Let him or her make three guesses. Then show your partner the object. Take turns playing the game.

When everyone is done, talk about how much easier it is to see things when they are in the light and not hidden. Talk about ways in which following Jesus is like seeing things in the light.

Jesus shows us the mercy of God.

We all sin. We all need God's mercy and forgiveness. Jesus calls us to **repent** for our sins. *To repent* means "to turn away from sin." We all need to repent, not just once, but over and over. We turn away from sin and ask God to help us live a good life. We need God's grace to heal us of sin and make us holy.

Faith Word

repent to turn away from sin

"See what love the Father has bestowed on us that we may be called the children of God."

1 John 3:1

Through Jesus' birth, God came to us and lived among us. Jesus shows us how to love and obey God. Jesus lived, died, and rose from the dead to free us from sin. He did this so we could live forever with God.

Our Baptism unites us with Christ as God's own children. In Baptism, we become members of the Body of Christ. We share in the life, Death, and Resurrection of Jesus. The grace of Christ helps us choose love over sin. In Jesus Christ, we have new life.

repent

 Show What You Know

Circle the correct term to complete the sentence.

1. God gives us _____ to help us live in his love and follow his commandments.

grades | gratitude | grace

2. We all need God's _____ and forgiveness.

mercy | money | magic

3. Grace _____ our friendship with God.

harms | heals | handles

4. To turn away from sin is to _____ .

pray | repent | remember

Partners in Faith

Saint John of the Cross

Saint John of the Cross was a Spanish priest and poet. He wrote beautiful poems about our friendship with God. Saint John had a vision of Jesus on the Cross. He drew a famous picture of his vision. Saint John was also a friend to Saint Teresa of Ávila.

 Learn more about the life of Saint John of the Cross.

Copyright © by William H. Sadlier, Inc. All rights reserved.

Mini-Task

God's grace helps us to love and care for ourselves and others. You will use what you know about grace to write a book. Your book will be used to teach younger children about God's grace.

Plan your book in the space below.

GOD'S GRACE

 Want to do more? Go to your Portfolio to continue this activity.

At Home

Jesus is a light, showing us the way to God. With your family, light a candle in the evening. Pray for the light of Jesus to shine in your family's life.

Copyright © by William H. Sadlier, Inc. All rights reserved.

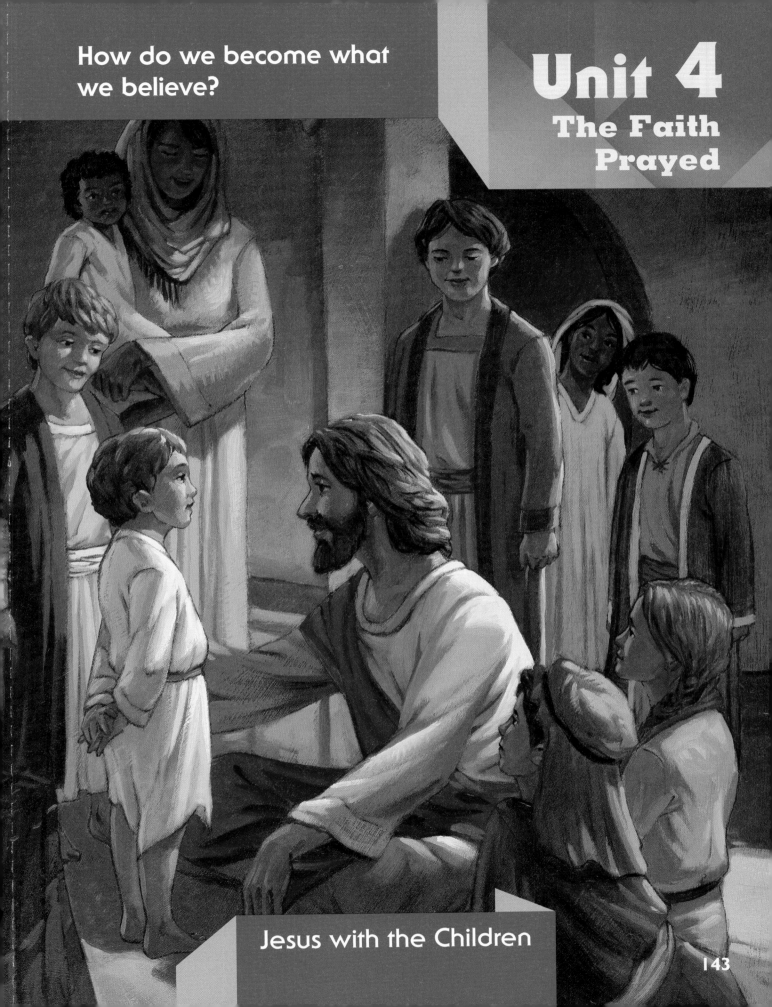

How do we become what we believe?

Jesus with the Children

Unit Prayer

Leader: Saint Thérèse of Lisieux felt that "a word or smile is often enough to put fresh life in a despondent soul." We know that Jesus is alive in our hearts and that he wants us to feel his love. Jesus also wants us to share his love by a kind word or even a smile.

Let us listen to how we can share the love of Jesus with others. Listen to the stories of missionary disciples among us.

Let us pray:
Dear Jesus, we know how much you love us. We can see it in all of creation and in the faces of those who love and care for us. Help us to feel your love.

All: Help us to feel your love.

Leader: Dear Jesus, we know that you want us to love each other. Help us to say a word that will make others feel loved. Help us to share your love.

All: Help us to share your love.

Leader: Dear Jesus, you smiled at your Mother, Mary, when you told her you loved her. Help us to smile at our family members when we tell them we love them. Help us to share your love.

All: Help us to share your love.

All sing: "We Are Marching"

 Unit Song: "We Are Marching," African/Traditional

Missionary Discipleship

How do you share Jesus' love with someone in your family or at school? A smile or a kind word is all you need to share.

What is prayer?

Jesus taught us to pray to God the Father as he did. When we pray, we raise our hearts and minds to God. We pray to God the Father in Jesus' name. God hears the prayers of all his people. God also speaks in our hearts. Talking to God and listening to God help us grow closer to him.

Go to the digital portal for a prayer of meditation.

"God has always called people to prayer."
Catechism of the Catholic Church, 2569

Prayer is talking and listening to God.

Before Jesus began to teach, he went into the desert to pray. He stayed there for many days, praying to his Father in heaven.

Jesus showed us that we all need to take quiet time to pray. **Prayer** is talking to God and listening to God. When we pray, we lift our hearts and minds to God.

We can talk to God about anything. We can tell God what we think and how we feel. We can ask for help or forgiveness. We can thank God for his many gifts. God always listens to us.

When we pray, we also listen to God. God is always speaking to our hearts. He speaks to us through the Church and the sacraments. He speaks to us through the Bible. God also speaks through the people who show his love.

Faith Word

prayer talking and listening to God

Where do I find a special place to pray?

Did You Know?

 Jesus teaches us how to pray.

Prayer is a special way God speaks to his people.

The Bible tells a story about a woman named Martha. She was Jesus' friend. Jesus went to visit Martha after her brother died. She told Jesus that she knew God would give him whatever he asked for. Jesus prayed to his Father and raised Martha's brother from the dead.

> "Jesus raised his eyes and said, 'Father, I thank you for hearing me. I know that you always hear me; but because of the crowd here I have said this, that they may believe that you sent me.'"
>
> John 11:41–42

Jesus showed that he talked to his Father and listened to him. God the Father always spoke to Jesus and listened to him, too.

God speaks to all of us and listens to us. Prayer is a special way God has always talked to and listened to his people.

God the Father loves us. He invites everyone to turn to him in prayer as Jesus did. When we pray, we show that we love God and want to be close to him.

Activity

Write one thing you want to say to God.

_____

_____

_____

What is one thing you would like to hear God say to you?

_____

_____

_____

God never stops listening to our prayers.

God the Father is always ready to listen to us. We can talk to God when we are lonely or afraid. We can tell God when we feel happy or excited. God wants us to talk to him no matter how we feel, in good times and bad times.

God also speaks to our hearts. When we pray, we take time to listen. It helps to have a quiet place to pray. Jesus went to the desert. You can go to a quiet room or somewhere outdoors that you like. You can pray before you fall asleep. Even a few minutes of quiet is enough to spend a little time with God in prayer. God is always listening!

Activity

Think about what would be a perfect prayer space for you. Do you like to pray indoors or outdoors? What things would you like to have around you to help you pray? Write about your favorite prayer space on the lines below.

_____

_____

_____

_____

We pray to God the Father, as Jesus taught us.

When we pray, we usually talk to and listen to God the Father. We pray to God the Father with Jesus, through Jesus, and in the name of Jesus. This shows that we love and trust God the Father as Jesus taught.

We can also pray to Jesus himself. When Jesus lived among us, many people went to him for help. They asked for healing and forgiveness. We can ask Jesus for help and healing, too. We can invite him into our hearts. We can ask him to send the Holy Spirit to help us.

We can also pray to God the Holy Spirit. When we need help, it is enough to simply pray "Come, Holy Spirit."

Faith Word

prayer

 Show What You Know

Circle the word that answers the question.

1. Who taught us to pray to God the Father as he did?

Joseph | Jesus

2. What word means talking to and listening to God?

prayer | praise

3. What do we make time to do when we pray?

listen | laugh

4. When is God ready to listen to us?

sometimes | always

Partners in Faith

Saint Genevieve

When Attila the Hun tried to invade Paris, Saint Genevieve told the people to pray and fast. She prayed with the people. The Huns did not attack. The city was saved.

 Learn more about the life of Saint Genevieve.

Copyright © by William H. Sadlier, Inc. All rights reserved.

How can I quiet my heart for prayer?

Mini-Task

Have you heard the phrase *Quiet yourself for prayer?* It simply means to settle ourselves down. We set a time to be calm and still. We open our thoughts and feelings to God. We get ready to talk to and listen to God in prayer.

Plan a prayer bell. Look at the outline of the bell. On the bell, write some words that help you quiet yourself.

You might write a short opening prayer to start each day of prayer.

Share your thoughts with a partner.

 Want to do more? Go to your Portfolio to continue this activity.

At Home

With your family, choose a special place to pray in or around your home. You may want to create and decorate one if you cannot find a place already set up for this. Spend some quiet time talking and listening to God together in that special place this week.

Copyright © by William H. Sadlier, Inc. All rights reserved.

Why do we pray?

Jesus showed us how to pray. We pray to become more like Jesus. Prayer helps us love God the Father and trust in him as Jesus did. Prayer helps us to follow Jesus and to do what he taught us. When we pray at all times and in all places, our love and trust in God grows.

Go to the digital portal for a prayer of praise.

"When you call me, and come and pray to me, I will listen to you."
Jeremiah 29:12

Jesus the Son of God showed us how to pray.

Jesus prayed to his Father often. His followers learned to pray by watching him and by listening to what Jesus taught. When Jesus returned to live with his Father in heaven, the Holy Spirit helped the Apostles pray.

The Apostles praised God together. They prayed for one another. They asked for courage to spread the word about Jesus. They prayed for the Church and her leaders.

Jesus wants us to pray together as the Apostles did. He gives us the Church to help us. The Holy Spirit guides the Church and teaches us to pray. Prayer helps us live as Jesus taught.

Why do I need to pray?

Did You Know?

 The Apostles came together in prayer.

Activity

Jesus showed us how to pray. What is your favorite way to pray? Talk with a partner about how you pray.

Prayer helps us love and trust in God.

Talking to the people we love helps us feel close to them. We like to know that someone is listening to us, even if we are not saying anything new or important.

God wants us to be close to him, too. He wants us to get to know him better. We grow closer to God when we pray. No matter how we pray, God is always with us.

God listens to all our prayers. He knows what we need and takes care of us. When we pray, we remember that God loves us as his own children. We learn to love and trust in God the Father, as Jesus did. Prayer helps us to become more like Jesus.

We can always pray.

Jesus prayed to God the Father often. He prayed with his family and with other people in their **worship** of God. As he grew older, Jesus also went off by himself to pray. He also prayed with his friends and disciples.

Jesus showed us that we can pray at any time. We need God always and everywhere. We can pray to God always and everywhere. We can pray when we are alone or with others in our community. We can use our own words or the prayers of the Church.

Jesus wants us to pray together with the whole Church. We do this by going to Mass and by saying other prayers of the Church. We also pray at home and in many other places.

We can pray even if we do not have much time. If we are busy or on our way somewhere, we can say very short prayers, like these:

- God, I love you.
- Jesus, be with me.
- Holy Spirit, help me.

For example, Saint Thérèse of Lisieux's favorite prayer was to simply say the name "Jesus" throughout the day. The more often we pray, the more we learn to remember that God is always with us.

Activity

Look at the clock. Choose one of the short prayers on this page. Print it in your clock.

Then decorate to complete your prayer clock.

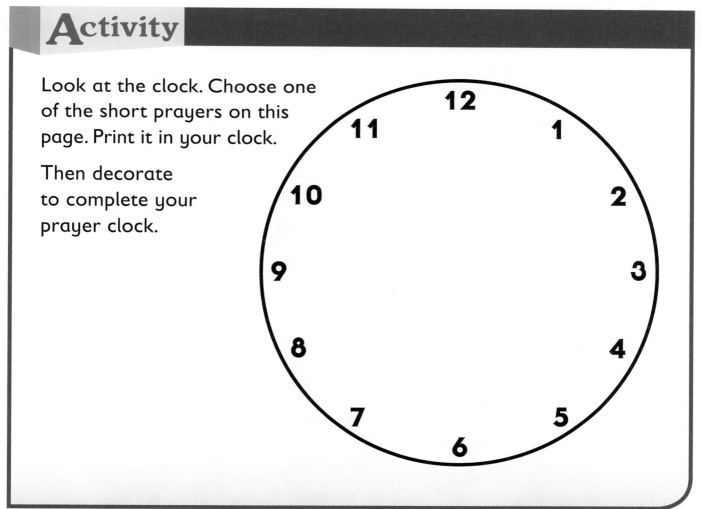

Our prayers show that we are God's children.

Jesus prayed often to God his Father. He prayed the night before he died. Jesus asked for help to do whatever God his Father wanted.

We all need God's help. We need help to obey God's commandments. We need help to follow Jesus. We need help to do the work of the Church. When we pray, we show that we are God's children and that we want to do his will.

There are many different ways to pray. We can praise God. We can tell God we are sorry for our sins. We can thank God for his loving care. We can ask God for the things we need. We can ask God to help other people.

All our prayers show that we are God's children and that we need God. They also remind us that God wants to be close to us.

Faith Word

worship

 Show What You Know

Circle the correct word to complete each sentence.

1. When we _____ God, we show that we love and honor him.

worship | watch for

2. The more often we pray, the more we remember that God is _____ with us.

sometimes | always

3. We grow closer to God when we _____ .

pray | play

4. The _____ Spirit guides the Church and teaches us to pray.

Holy | Happy

Partners in Faith

Saint Rose Philippine Duchesne

Saint Rose Philippine Duchesne came to America to help Native Americans. She often prayed with the people. Saint Rose spent so much time in prayer that she was called the Woman Who Prays Always.

 Learn more about the life of Saint Rose Philippine Duchesne.

Copyright © by William H. Sadlier, Inc. All rights reserved.

Lesson 17
Portfolio

Who helps me pray?

Mini-Task

As Catholics, we pray with others.

At the top of each figure, print the first name of a person who helps you to pray. Draw the faces to look like the people you have chosen.

 Want to do more? Go to your Portfolio to continue this activity.

At Home

When we pray, we pray with the whole Church, including the saints who are in heaven now. Is anyone in your family named after a saint? Does anyone in your family have a favorite saint? Say a prayer to one of these saints.

160 **WITNESS**

Copyright © by William H. Sadlier, Inc. All rights reserved.

How do we pray?

Jesus taught us how to pray. We should pray every day. The Holy Spirit helps us. Like Jesus, we pray with our thoughts, words, and actions, both silently and out loud. We pray alone, with our families, and with the Church. We pray in many ways. We praise, thank, and bless God. We also pray for ourselves and others.

Go to the digital portal for a prayer of petition.

"We praise you, we bless you, we adore you, we glorify you, we give you thanks for your great glory, Lord God, heavenly King, O God, almighty Father." Gloria, Order of Mass

Jesus taught us how to pray.

Jesus taught us to pray to God the Father. The Holy Spirit helps us to bless, praise, and thank God for his gifts. We ask God to help us and others. We ask for forgiveness for our sins. Jesus gave us a prayer that includes all these different ways to pray. You will learn about the **Lord's Prayer** later in your book.

Faith Word

Lord's Prayer the prayer Jesus taught his followers

Like Jesus, we pray with words and actions, both silently and out loud. Sometimes we do all these things together. At Mass, we listen to a reading from the Gospel. Before the reading, we pray out loud: "Glory to you, O Lord." We pray silently for the Word of God to stay always on our minds, on our lips, and in our hearts.

Who taught me how to pray?

Did You Know?

God is all around us.

Jesus taught his disciples to pray.

Jesus' disciples learned to pray as Jesus taught. They gave what they learned to the whole Church. The Holy Spirit also guided the Church to pray in new ways.

One of the Church's most important prayers is the Hail Mary. In this prayer, we honor Mary, the mother of Jesus. We say that Mary is special because she was chosen to become the Mother of God's Son. We also ask Mary to pray for us always.

The Hail Mary

Hail Mary, full of grace,
the Lord is with you!
Blessed are you among
women, and blessed is the
fruit of your womb, Jesus.
Holy Mary, Mother of God,
pray for us sinners,
now and at the hour
of our death.
Amen.

 Hail Mary

We pray the Hail Mary often when we pray the Rosary. The Rosary is a prayer of devotion in honor of Mary. When we pray the Rosary, we use special beads. We think about the lives of Mary and Jesus. You can learn how to pray the Rosary by looking in the back of your book.

Activity

Color the picture of the rosary.

Show your picture to a friend.
Then pray the Hail Mary together.

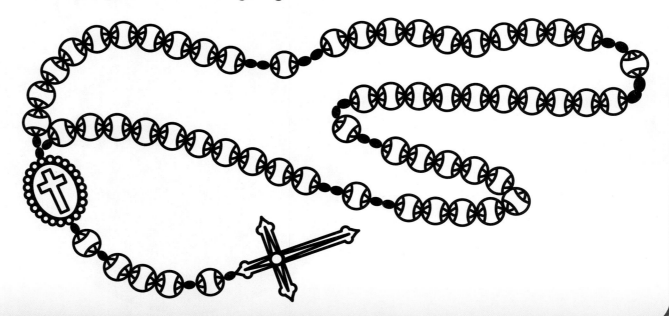

Faith Word

psalms songs of praise from the Bible

The Church prays together at special times.

The Church celebrates the sacraments as well as holy people and events. Some parishes also gather to pray the **psalms** at morning and evening prayer. Psalms are songs of praise from the Bible.

 "Shout joyfully to the LORD, all you lands;
serve the LORD with gladness;
come before him with joyful song." Psalm 100:1–2

Activity

A psalm is a prayer that is like a poem or a song. With a friend, write a psalm giving thanks to God for all he has given you. Write one line and then have your friend write the next one. Use the words below to help you start your prayer.

thank you   **gift**   **love**   **God**

Share your psalm with the group.

Jesus prayed in many ways.

Jesus prayed with words from the Bible and in his own words. He prayed silently and out loud. Jesus often spent time alone with God the Father in prayer.

We pray in many ways, just as Jesus did. We pray in our own words. We use prayers we learn at home, in school, and in our parish. We pray out loud and silently to ourselves. We can pray while reading the Bible or looking at a holy image. Sometimes we pray by just sitting quietly and remembering that God is with us.

God listens to all our prayers, even those we say silently in our hearts. What matters most is that we lift our hearts and minds to God when we pray.

Faith Words

Lord's Prayer   psalms

 Show What You Know

Circle the correct term to complete each sentence.

1. The _____ is the prayer Jesus taught his followers.

Last Prayer | Lord's Prayer | Leaving Prayer

2. _____ are songs of praise from the Bible.

Petitions | Liturgies | Psalms

3. We lift our hearts and _____ to God when we pray.

hands | minds | eyes

Partners in Faith

Saint Bernadette Soubirous

Mary appeared to Saint Bernadette, a poor French girl, in a town called Lourdes. Mary called herself the Immaculate Conception. She told Bernadette to pray the Rosary. Many people visit the shrine at Lourdes every year to pray for healing.

 Learn more about the life of Saint Bernadette Soubirous.

Copyright © by William H. Sadlier, Inc. All rights reserved.

How do I pray?

Mini-Task

In this lesson, you learned that there are many ways to pray. We can pray many different kinds of prayers.

- I can pray a prayer that I have learned in *Christ In Us*.

- I can pray a prayer that I learned with my family.

- I can pray a prayer that I read in the Bible.

- I can pray a prayer I hear at Mass.

- I can pray a prayer in my own words.

Plan a prayer box for your room at home. Circle three of the suggestions that you will use to write three prayers.

With a partner, share why you chose the prayers in your prayer box plan.

 Want to do more? Go to your Portfolio to continue this activity.

Together, pray the Hail Mary as a family every evening this week. If you have a rosary at home, learn together how to pray the Rosary and pray it before you go to Mass this week.

Copyright © by William H. Sadlier, Inc. All rights reserved.

Jesus shows us how important prayer is. Jesus prayed at all times. The Holy Spirit helps us to pray, even when it is difficult. Our families teach us how to pray. The Church and the Bible help us to pray as Jesus did. Our prayers show that we believe in God and want to follow Jesus.

Go to the digital portal for a *Lectio* and *Visio Divina* prayer.

"O God, our refuge and our strength,
hear the prayers of your Church,
for you yourself are the source of all devotion."
Universal Prayer, *Roman Missal*

The Church is the Body of Christ.

God gives us the Church to help us pray. The Church is the Body of Christ, the one family of God. When we pray with the Church, we pray with the living, with those who have died and are being purified before entering heaven, and with the saints in heaven. Whoever and wherever we are, we are one Body in Christ.

The whole Church prays together. We pray for God to bless and be with all those who are living. We ask God to welcome into eternal life those who have died. We ask the saints to pray for us.

Prayer helps the Body of Christ to be holy. Prayer shows that we love and believe in God and want to follow Jesus.

Who prays for me?

Did You Know?

Holiness is sharing God's love by the way we live.

Activity

We can ask the saints in heaven to pray for us. Ask one of the saints you have learned about this year to help and pray for you. Write the saint's name on the line.

_____

Ask your friends to share the name of the saints they chose. Together, ask the saints to "Pray for us."

We learn prayers from the Bible and at church.

The Church helps us to pray. The Bible helps us, too. Many of the Bible readings you hear at church were written before Jesus was born. Jesus listened to those same readings when he prayed with his **community**.

Faith Word

community a group of people joined together by where they live or other things they have in common

Other readings from the Bible were written after Jesus returned to his Father in heaven. Jesus is the center of the Bible. Readings about Jesus are the most important part of God's Word to us.

The Church prays with the Bible as Jesus did. Many of the prayers we say at church come from the Bible. For instance, we sing "Glory to God in the highest" just as angels did at the birth of Jesus (see Luke 2:14).

We also pray words from the Bible during the Eucharist.
The priest prays in the words of Jesus at the Last Supper:

> "Then he took the bread, said the blessing, broke it, and gave it to them, saying, 'This is my body, which will be given for you; do this in memory of me.'" (Luke 22:19)

Activity

Use the words below to fill in the blanks in the sentences of this prayer from the Mass.

peace   glory   bless   Father

Glory to God in the highest,

and on earth _____ to people of good will.

We praise you,

we _____ you,

we adore you,

we glorify you,

we give you thanks for your great _____ ,

Lord God, heavenly King,

O God, almighty _____ .

Our parents usually teach us to pray.

Our families are the first place we learn to pray. The Bible tells us that Jesus and his family traveled every year to celebrate religious holidays in the holy city of Jerusalem (see Luke 2:41). They also prayed in their home town with their own community.

The most important way for families to pray together is to go to Mass every Sunday. There are many other times for families to pray. Help your family get into the habit of praying before meals and trips. Ask God to help family members who are sick, traveling, or starting something new. Pray from the Bible together.

By praying together, families help each other's faith grow strong.

Jesus shows us how to pray.

The Bible tells us that Jesus prayed to his Father at all times. He prayed when he was baptized and when he healed people. Jesus prayed at the Last Supper and on the Cross. Jesus trusted that God the Father always heard him.

Jesus loved his Father. He showed us how to trust in God. Jesus even prayed to God the Father when he was suffering and dying. He said: "Father, forgive them, they know not what they do" (Luke 23:34).

It is not always easy for us to pray. Sometimes we might feel bored or restless. We show our love for God when we keep trying. Jesus lifted his whole heart and mind to God the Father when he prayed. Praying like Jesus helps us have even more trust in God.

Faith Word

community

 Show What You Know

Use the words below to complete the sentences.

Mass   **holy**   **Bible**   **families**   **community**

1. The _____ tells us that Jesus prayed to his Father at all times.

2. The most important way for families to pray together is to join their parish for _____ every Sunday.

3. Prayer helps the Body of Christ to be _____ .

4. Our _____ are the first place we learn to pray.

5. Jesus' family prayed in their home town with their _____ .

Partners in Faith

Saint Ignatius of Antioch

Saint Ignatius of Antioch was the first to use the words *Catholic Church* in writing. He wrote many letters to the early Church. He died for his faith in the year 108.

 Learn more about the life of Saint Ignatius of Antioch.

Copyright © by William H. Sadlier, Inc. All rights reserved.

Whom do I pray with?

Mini-Task

Jesus prayed with his family and with his community. We are part of Jesus' community, the Church. Jesus is with us when we pray.

Imagine you are a reporter doing a story about community and prayer. Interview three people using the questions below.

• Who is part of your church community?

• How does your church community help you pray?

• What prayer do you pray with your church community?

Share your answers with a partner. How are the answers alike? How are they different?

 Want to do more? Go to your Portfolio to continue this activity.

Review some of the prayer ideas in this lesson. Ask your family about their favorite ways to pray. Choose one way to pray together now.

Copyright © by William H. Sadlier, Inc. All rights reserved.

Why is the Lord's Prayer called the perfect prayer?

Jesus showed us how to live by everything he said and did. To help us love God and others as Jesus did, he taught us to call God our Father. When we pray the Our Father, which is the Lord's Prayer, we honor God the Father and show that we trust in his care for us.

 Go to the digital portal for a traditional prayer.

"Prayer is the living relationship of the children of God with their Father."
Catechism of the Catholic Church, 2565

The Lord's Prayer shows us how we should pray.

God the Father has only one divine Son, Jesus Christ. In Baptism, we become God's adopted sons and daughters. God's only Son, Jesus, taught us to call God our Father when we pray.

Jesus taught his followers the Lord's Prayer. It is also called the Our Father. When we pray the Lord's Prayer, we praise God. We ask him to help us obey his commandments.

The Lord's Prayer is the perfect prayer because it helps us remember everything Jesus taught. It helps us to follow the Great Commandment. It helps us love God and our neighbor. The Lord's Prayer is central to the Church because it helps us love God and live as Jesus taught.

What would I like to ask of God?

Did You Know?

We can see examples of Jesus' teachings everywhere.

Jesus taught his disciples a special prayer.

Jesus' disciples saw how important prayer was to Jesus. The Bible tells us: "He was praying in a certain place, and when he had finished, one of his disciples said to him, 'Lord, teach us to pray'" (Luke 11:1). Jesus taught them this special prayer.

The Lord's Prayer

Our Father, who art in heaven,
hallowed be thy name;
thy kingdom come,
thy will be done on earth as it is in heaven.
Give us this day our daily bread,
and forgive us our trespasses,
as we forgive those who trespass against us;
and lead us not into temptation,
but deliver us from evil.
Amen.

The Lord's Prayer

When we pray the Lord's Prayer, we are united with God the Father and with his Son, Jesus Christ.

Activity

Write what you think each of these parts from the Lord's Prayer means.

Our Father _____ ,

who art in heaven _____ ,

hallowed be thy name _____ .

We pray to God in the Lord's Prayer.

God our Father wants us to tell him our needs when we pray. We also pray to show God that we love him and that we want to obey him.

We begin the Lord's Prayer by praising God and telling him that we trust him as our Father.

The First Part of the Lord's Prayer	What We Ask
Our Father, who art in heaven,	We praise God as our loving Father.
hallowed be thy name;	We respect the holy name of God.
thy kingdom come; thy will be done on earth as it is in heaven.	We ask that all people will share in God's love. We ask that all things happen just as God wants them to.

When we pray the Lord's Prayer, we ask that someday God's love will be active everywhere in the world. God's reign over sin, suffering, and death is called the **Kingdom of God**. God loves the world and all people he has made. Even so, all people sin, suffer, and die. We believe that when God's Kingdom fully comes, all people will know and share in God's love and life forever.

Faith Word

Kingdom of God God's reign over sin, suffering, and death

Activity

Match each line of the Lord's Prayer with the correct action.

hallowed be thy name;   ask

Give us this day our daily bread;   confess

and forgive us our trespasses.   adore

We show our trust in God in the Lord's Prayer.

In the second part of the Lord's Prayer, we pray for ourselves. Jesus taught us that we can turn to God, our loving Father, whenever we are in need.

The Second Part of the Lord's Prayer	What We Ask
Give us this day our daily bread;	We ask God to give us what we need to live as he made us.
and forgive us our trespasses as we forgive those who trespass against us	We ask God to forgive our sins. We remember that we must forgive others.
and lead us not into temptation,	We ask for God's help to avoid doing anything sinful.
but deliver us from evil.	We ask God to keep us safe from everything that goes against his love.

When we pray the Lord's Prayer, we show that we need God. We also show that we trust God the Father to take care of us and to help us live as Jesus taught.

Faith Word

Kingdom of God

 Show What You Know

In your own words, write a definition for the term.

Kingdom of God

_____

_____

Answer the question.

What do we show God when we pray the Lord's Prayer?

_____

_____

Partners in Faith

Saint Juan Diego

Saint Juan Diego was a native Mexican. He and his wife became Christians. As part of their education, they learned the Our Father. Later, Mary appeared to Juan and called herself Our Lady of Guadalupe.

 Learn more about the life of Saint Juan Diego.

Copyright © by William H. Sadlier, Inc. All rights reserved.

Mini-Task

Jesus taught his followers the Lord's Prayer. The Lord's Prayer taught Jesus' followers how to pray.

Imagine that you have been asked to help teach a prayer to a group of younger children.

Plan a short video. You are going to inspire other children to pray the Lord's Prayer. Your video should teach the viewers what the Lord's Prayer tells us about God and ourselves.

To begin, design or write one way the Lord's Prayer teaches us about God.

Share with a partner.

 Want to do more? Go to your Portfolio to continue this activity.

Practice praying the Our Father every day with your family. Take turns saying the lines aloud. If you are able to, record your family praying the Our Father and send the audio or video to a grandparent or friend.

Copyright © by William H. Sadlier, Inc. All rights reserved.

Liturgical Calendar

DEC
JAN
NOV
FEB
OCT
MAR
SEP
APR
AUG
MAY
JUL
JUN

Advent
Christmas
Ordinary Time
Lent
Triduum
Easter
Ordinary Time

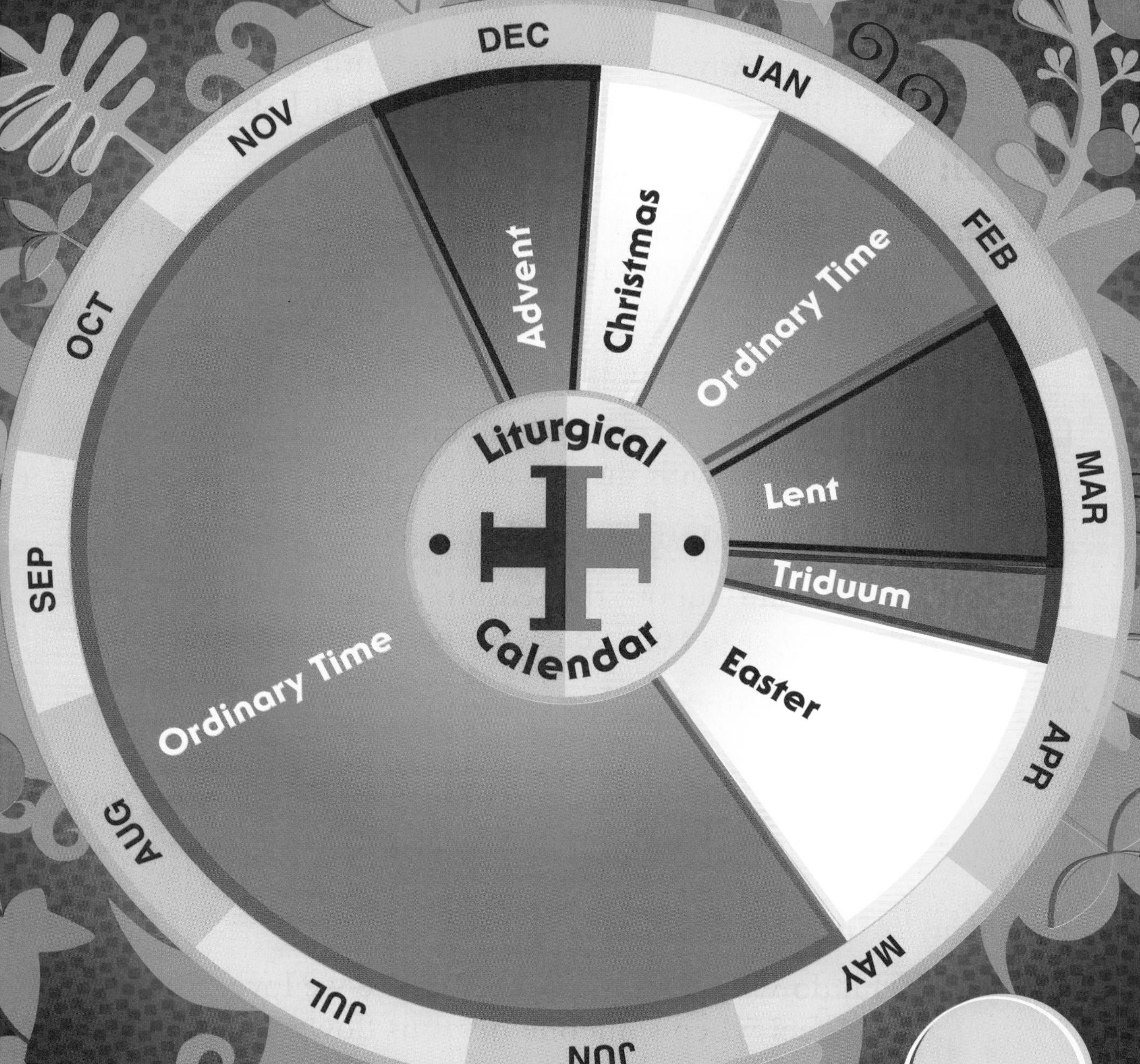

Unit Prayer

Leader: Saint Thérèse of Lisieux shows us how to use the beauty of creation to find God's love for us. She compared us to flowers, all different, yet all special and wonderful.

When we are at Mass throughout the year, we celebrate the love of God in many different ways. Let us thank God for his love for us:

O God, in Advent and Christmas, with evergreens and poinsettias, we thank you for the gift of Jesus.

All: Thank you for the gift of Jesus.

Leader: O God, in Lent and Easter, with palm branches and lilies, we praise you for the love that Jesus gave us and for his Resurrection.

All: Thank you for the gift of Jesus.

Leader: O God, at Pentecost, with all kinds of red flowers, we are filled with the fire of your Holy Spirit.

All: Thank you for the gift of Jesus.

Leader: O God, throughout the seasons of the year, with all the plants, we raise our voices to thank you for your love.

All sing: "We Will Praise You"

 Unit Song: "We Will Praise You," Tom Kendzia/OCP

Missionary Discipleship

Why do we give flowers to someone we love? How do we feel when someone gives us flowers? Why are there different kinds of flowers at Mass?

How do we celebrate Jesus Christ?

Lesson 21

Church Year

"Give to the LORD, you families of nations, give to the LORD glory and might."

1 Chronicles 16:28

 **Prayer**

Gathering Prayer

Leader: With grateful hearts, we pray with the different seasons of the Church year. We call the Church year the liturgical year.

Thank you, Lord, for the seasons of the Church year.

All: Thank you, Lord, for the seasons of the Church year.

Leader: Each season helps us to love God more fully. Thank you, Lord, for the seasons of the Church year.

All: Thank you, Lord, for the seasons of the Church year.

Leader: Each season helps us know the life and teachings of Jesus and the power of the Holy Spirit. Let us give thanks for the Church year.

All: Thank you, Lord, for the seasons of the Church year.

Activity

In small groups, talk about the seasons of the Church year. What things stay the same all year?

The Church celebrates Jesus' life and work all year.

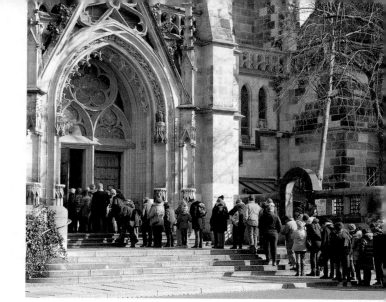

The Church gives us liturgical seasons throughout the year. These seasons help us celebrate the life of Jesus. We also celebrate special people and events during the Church year.

The season of Advent prepares us to celebrate Christmas. Christmas shows us the wonder of Jesus' birth. Lent prepares us to celebrate Easter. The season of Easter shows us the wonder of the Resurrection.

The season of Ordinary Time celebrates Jesus' life. It reminds us that Jesus calls everyone to follow him.

The Church celebrates the Mass every day. But some special days in the liturgical year honor Mary, the Mother of Jesus. We honor other saints' days, too. The most special day of all is Sunday, when we celebrate Jesus' Resurrection. We go to Mass every Sunday.

Church Year

Did You Know?

 Each day of the Church year is unique.

Activity

Put a star next to your favorite season of the Church year.

Advent   **Christmas**

Ordinary Time   **Lent**

Easter

Readers Theater

Jesus Feeds Five Thousand

Matthew 14:13–21

Roles: Narrator 1, Narrator 2, Narrator 3, Disciple 1, Disciple 2, Jesus

The Church year helps us remember Jesus' life. In this story, we hear about the many people who came to see Jesus. He healed the sick and fed everyone with just five loaves of bread and two fish.

Narrator 1: Jesus heard that John the Baptist had died. John was the cousin of Jesus.

Narrator 2: Jesus went to a place where he could be alone.

Narrator 3: But people found out where he was and came to see him.

Narrator 1: His heart was filled with love for the people. He cured those who were sick.

Narrator 2: The people stayed with Jesus for a long time. It was getting late in the day.

Disciple 1: Jesus, tell the people to go home. It is getting late.

Disciple 2: The people are hungry. There is no food here for everyone.

Jesus: "There is no need for them to go away; give them some food yourselves" (Matthew 14:16).

Disciple 1: "Five loaves and two fish are all we have here" (Matthew 14:17).

Jesus: "Bring them here to me" (Matthew 14:18).

Narrator 2: Jesus took the five loaves of bread and the two fish. He said a prayer to his Father in heaven.

Jesus: Give the food to the people to eat.

Disciple 2: There is enough for everyone!

Narrator 1: Everyone had bread and fish to eat. No one was hungry that day.

Narrator 2: The people who came to see Jesus were fed.

Narrator 3: There were more than five thousand men, women, and children there!

How do I remember Jesus all year?

Mini-Task

The seasons of the Church year help us remember and celebrate Jesus. There are seven seasons of the Church year. Every season has special colors, signs, and symbols. Signs and symbols help us to celebrate.

An icon is a type of symbol that uses a picture to represent something. Each time you learn about a season of the Church year, you will design an icon for it.

Design a symbol for the entire Church year. Choose colors and a picture to use as your icon.

Share your icon with a friend. Explain why you designed it to look the way it does.

The Church Year

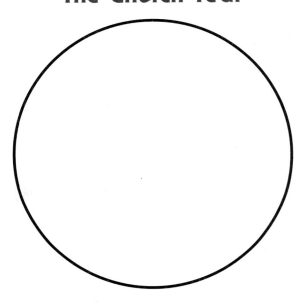

 Want to do more? Go to your Portfolio to continue this activity.

At Home

Talk as a family about some seasonal traditions you have. Ask family members if they would like to start any new faith traditions this year.

Copyright © by William H. Sadlier, Inc. All rights reserved.

Why does Jesus come to save us?

Advent

"Prepare the way of the Lord, make straight his paths." Luke 3:4

Gathering Prayer

Leader: As we celebrate the season of Advent, we thank God for this special time when we prepare to celebrate the birth of Jesus.

O God, we are blessed to know your Son, Jesus.

All: (*Touch your head with your hands.*)

We are blessed to know Jesus.

Leader: We are blessed to see him in one another through our loving and caring actions.

All: (*Touch your eyes with your hands.*)

We are blessed to see Jesus.

Leader: We are blessed to hear his words in Scripture and in the kind words we share with one another.

All: (*Touch your ears with your hands.*)

We are blessed to hear Jesus.

Leader: The light of Jesus shines in you!

All: (*Point to the person next to you.*)

The light of Jesus shines in you! Amen.

Activity

Draw something you can do to get ready for Jesus' birth at Christmas.

We show patience as we wait for Jesus.

Advent means "to come" or "is coming." During the season of Advent, we prepare to celebrate the coming of Jesus.

We show patience as we wait. *Patience* means "waiting peacefully for something to happen." When we are patient, we wait without getting upset when things take a long time.

Jesus is the greatest sign of God's love. We wait patiently for Jesus because he loves us.

We can be patient in many ways as we wait for Jesus. We can say an extra prayer every day to keep our thoughts on Jesus. We can be kind and helpful to a friend or family member.

We can work harder at taking care of others who need our help. We pay attention to Jesus, whom we see in the love and goodness of others.

Did You Know?

 Patience pays off.

Activity

Circle the ways we can wait patiently. Mark an X on actions that do not show patience.

pay attention   pray   **be bossy**   ignore

complain   think of Jesus   help others

Advent Prayer Ritual

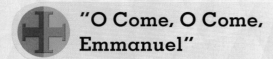 "O Come, O Come, Emmanuel"

Leader: Lord God, we joyfully await the coming of your Son and our Savior, Jesus Christ. Let your love be with us this season. The light of this wreath reminds us of the light of Christ. Jesus shines in our hearts and in the world!

In Advent, we prepare our hearts to celebrate the birth of Jesus at Christmas. Let us pray: "Prepare the way of the Lord!"

All: Prepare the way of the Lord!

Leader: Let us listen to a reading from the prophet Isaiah:
"A voice proclaims:
In the wilderness prepare the way of the LORD!
Make straight in the wasteland a highway for our God!
Every valley shall be lifted up,
every mountain and hill made low; . . .
Then the glory of the LORD shall be revealed,
and all . . . shall see it together" (Isaiah 40:3–5).

All: Prepare the way of the Lord!

Leader: Lord Jesus, prepare in our hearts a place for your return.

All: Prepare the way of the Lord!

Leader: Jesus, open our eyes so that we may see you in the faces of each other.

All: Prepare the way of the Lord!

Leader: Jesus, help us to remember that Advent is a gift to us. It is a time that helps us prepare for the season of Christmas. Help us to make Advent special with our prayers and good works. We prepare the way for your coming at Christmas.

All: Prepare the way of the Lord!

How can I prepare to celebrate the birth of Jesus?

Mini-Task

The first season of the Church year is Advent. Advent helps us get ready for Jesus! During Advent, we light a special wreath with pink and purple candles. Purple is the color of Advent.

Design an icon for Advent. An icon is a type of symbol that uses a picture to represent something. Choose colors and a picture to use as your icon.

Share your icon with a friend. Can your friend guess which season it symbolizes? Explain why you designed it to look the way it does.

Advent

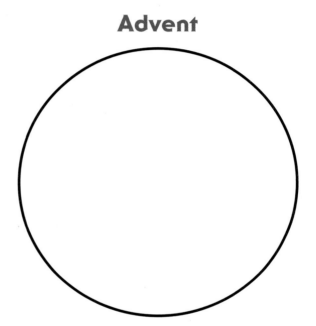

 Want to do more? Go to your Portfolio to continue this activity.

At  Home

With your family, talk about ways you can show patience and kindness to others this Advent.

Copyright © by William H. Sadlier, Inc. All rights reserved.

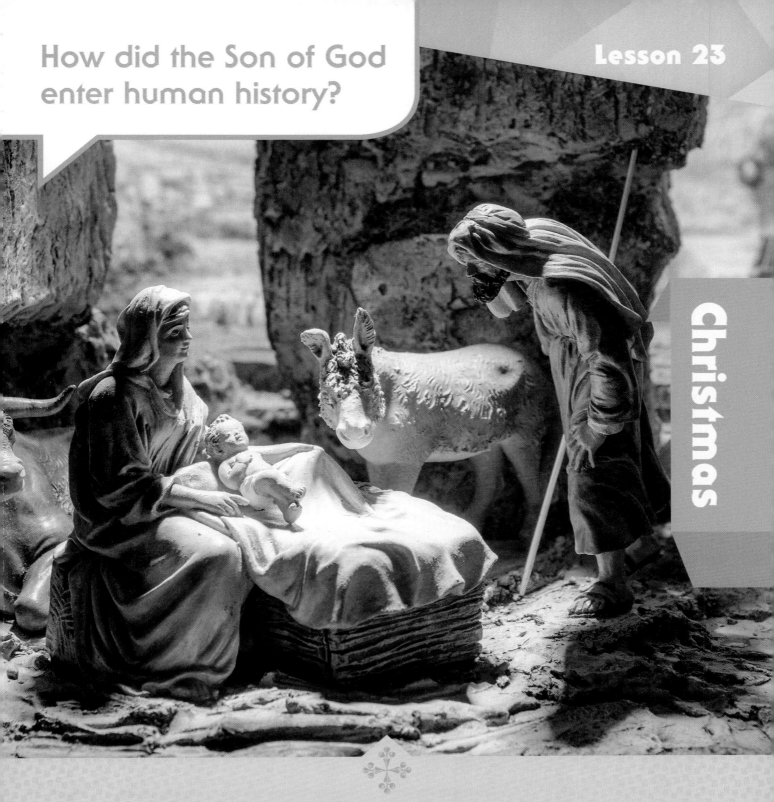

How did the Son of God enter human history?

Christmas

"I proclaim to you good news of great joy that will be for all the people."

Luke 2:10

Gathering Prayer

Leader: We give thanks for the beautiful season of Christmas. We give thanks for the gift of Jesus, who fills our lives with love and peace.

Let us sing: "O come let us adore him, O come let us adore him, O come let us adore him, Christ the Lord."

All: "O come let us adore him, O come let us adore him, O come let us adore him, Christ the Lord."

Leader: With the angels who sang with Mary, Joseph, and the shepherds, we sing:

All: "O come let us adore him, O come let us adore him, O come let us adore him, Christ the Lord."

Leader: We are filled with joy because Jesus is born in our hearts! Let us sing:

All: "O come let us adore him, O come let us adore him, O come let us adore him, Christ the Lord."

Activity

Do you have a favorite Christmas song about Jesus? Teach the song to your group.

Jesus is the Son of God and the Son of Mary.

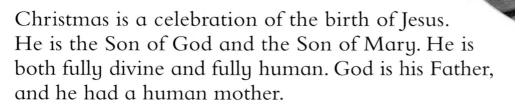

Christmas Day is so important that the Church celebrates it for eight days. The celebration begins with the birth of Jesus on Christmas Day, December 25. This is the Feast of the Nativity. Eight days later, on January 1, we celebrate Mary, the Mother of God.

Christmas is a celebration of the birth of Jesus. He is the Son of God and the Son of Mary. He is both fully divine and fully human. God is his Father, and he had a human mother.

On January 1, we celebrate Mary as the Mother of God. We respect and love Mary, the Mother of Jesus. Mary is a mother to us, too. She wants us to be close to her Son, Jesus.

Did You Know?

 Mary is Jesus' Mother and ours, too.

Activity

Work with a partner to list the members in Jesus' family.

_____

_____

_____

_____

Christmas Prayer Ritual

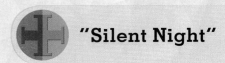 **"Silent Night"**

Leader: The beautiful season of Christmas, the birth of Jesus, is a season of joy and gifts. Jesus, God the Father's greatest gift to humanity, was born to save humankind from sin and death.

When we pray in front of the manger, we see Jesus as a baby with his Mother, Mary, and his foster father, Joseph. God gave Joseph care over Mary and his only begotten Son, Jesus. What an amazing responsibility!

"Hark the herald angels sing, glory to the newborn king."

All: (*Sing*) "Hark the herald angels sing, glory to the newborn king."

Leader: Listen to a Scripture reading from Luke 2:8–12:

"Now there were shepherds in that region living in the fields and keeping the night watch over their flock. The angel of the Lord appeared to them . . . and they were struck with great fear. The angel said to them, 'Do not be afraid; for behold, I proclaim to you good news of great joy that will be for all the people . . . . A savior has been born for you who is Messiah and Lord. And this will be a sign for you: you will find an infant wrapped in swaddling clothes and lying in a manger.'"

All: (*Sing*)"Hark the herald angels sing, glory to the newborn king."

Leader: I proclaim to you good news of great joy: Christ the Lord is born for us.

All: (*Sing*)"Hark the herald angels sing, glory to the newborn king."

Leader: At Mass, we sing the song of the angels:"Glory to God in the highest, and on earth peace to people of good will."

All: (*Sing*)"Hark the herald angels sing, glory to the newborn king."

Leader: Jesus came to offer the gift of his peace to us. Let us now offer the sign of Christ's peace to each other.

(Offer a sign of peace by shaking hands with those around you.)

All: (*Sing*) "Hark the herald angels sing, glory to the newborn king."

How is Jesus God's greatest gift to me?

Mini-Task

Christmas is a time to celebrate the birth of Jesus. We hear about the angel who told the shepherds that Jesus was born. We learn about the wise men, who brought gifts to newborn Jesus.

During the Christmas season, the church is decorated in white and gold.

Design an icon for Christmas. An icon is a type of symbol that uses a picture to represent something. Choose colors and a picture to use as your icon.

Share your icon with a friend. Can your friend guess which season it symbolizes? Explain why you designed it to look the way it does.

Christmas

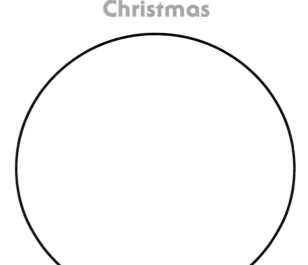

 Want to do more? Go to your Portfolio to continue this activity.

At Home

As a family, make an ornament or another decoration to celebrate Jesus' birth. Hang your ornament or decoration in your home.

Copyright © by William H. Sadlier, Inc. All rights reserved.

How are we called to repentance today?

Lent

"Whoever drinks the water I shall give will never thirst." John 4:14

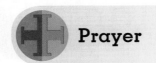 **Prayer**

Gathering Prayer

Leader: During Lent, we take time to know more about how much Jesus loves us. We hear about the ways Jesus asked his disciples to follow his words. We learn how Jesus was to suffer and die for our sins. We do special actions that help us remember Jesus' love for us. Let us pray:

Jesus, open our hearts to your love.

All: Jesus, open our hearts to your love.

Leader: Help us to spend more time in prayer:

All: Jesus, open our hearts to your love.

Leader: Teach us to be kind and helpful to others:

All: Jesus, open our hearts to your love.

Leader: Show us how we can love you more each day of Lent:

All: Jesus, open our hearts to your love.

Leader: Let us be ready to celebrate your sacred Triduum and the great feast of Easter:

All: Jesus, open our hearts to your love.

Activity

Think about a way you can open your heart to Jesus' love during Lent. Share your way with the group.

_____

Lent brings us closer to Jesus.

We think about Jesus in a special way during Lent. At Mass, we hear about three signs that Jesus gave us to know how much God loves us.

The first of the signs is water. Jesus is the living water. Jesus takes care of us and helps us grow the same way water helps flowers grow.

The second of the signs is light. Jesus gives light to all people, especially those who are lost or in darkness.

The third of these signs is life. Jesus gives new life to all who follow him.

Water, light, and life are all signs of the Sacrament of Baptism. We are baptized in water. We are given a lighted candle. In Baptism, we are given new life: we now share in God's own life.

During Lent, we celebrate the gift of Baptism. This gift from God lasts our whole life.

Did You Know?

We need to nourish our faith.

Activity

Work in groups of three to act out the three signs that Jesus gave us to know how much God loves us: water, light, and life. Have other groups guess which signs your team members are acting out.

Readers Theater

Jesus Enters Jerusalem

Mark 11:1–11

Roles: Narrator 1, Narrator 2, Disciple 1, Disciple 2, Disciple 3, Jesus, People (can be a small group or everyone)

Jesus came to Jerusalem to celebrate the Passover with his disciples.

Narrator 1: Jesus and his disciples were near Jerusalem.

Narrator 2: He talked to the disciples who were with him.

Jesus: Go into the town. Take the colt tied to a tree that you find there.

Disciple 1: What if someone asks: "Why are you taking that colt?"

Jesus: Tell them that the Master has need of the colt. He will bring it back to them.

Narrator 1: The disciples brought the colt to Jesus.

Narrator 2: They put their coats on the colt. Jesus sat on it.

Narrator 1: The disciples led Jesus into town. He was riding on the colt.

Narrator 2: There were many people along the road. They said:

People: "Hosanna! Blessed is he who comes in the name of the Lord!" (Mark 11:9)

Narrator 1: The people put their own coats on the road. The colt walked on the coats.

Narrator 2: The people waved leafy branches as Jesus came by.

People: "Blessed is the kingdom of our father David that is to come!
Hosanna in the highest!" (Mark 11:10)

Disciple 2: Jesus, the people speak to you like a king!

Disciple 3: They think you are a prophet!

Narrator 1: When Jesus came to the Temple, he went inside.

Narrator 2: He stayed at the Temple for a while. Then he went away with the disciples.

How can I be closer to Jesus?

Mini-Task

Lent is a time to be closer to Jesus.

Purple is the color of Lent. The church is decorated in purple, and the priest wears purple vestments.

During Lent, we learn about how Jesus gave us signs of his love. We remember to pray and to be kind and generous to others.

Design an icon for Lent. Choose colors and a picture to use as your icon.

Share your icon with a friend. Can your friend guess which season it symbolizes? Explain why you designed it to look the way it does.

Lent

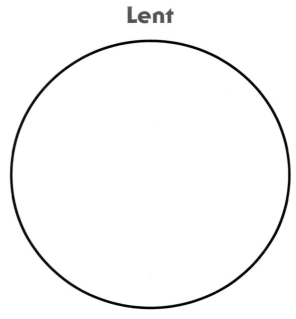

 Want to do more? Go to your Portfolio to continue this activity.

Light a candle and pray tonight as a family that you will show the light of Christ to the world. If members of your family have candles they were given at Baptism, use one of those candles.

Copyright © by William H. Sadlier, Inc. All rights reserved.

Why did Jesus die on the Cross and rise again?

Triduum

"He was brought to life in the spirit."

1 Peter 3:18

 **Prayer**

Gathering Prayer

Leader: The three days of the Triduum are beautiful reminders of God the Father's greatest gift, his Son, Jesus.

Dear Jesus, help us to love you more deeply.

All: Dear Jesus, help us to love you more deeply.

Leader: On Holy Thursday, washing feet is a reminder that we should serve one another; the Eucharist is a sacrifice and a call to service.

All: Dear Jesus, help us to love you more deeply.

Leader: On Good Friday, we remember the story of your suffering and Death on the Cross.

All: Dear Jesus, help us to love you more deeply.

Leader: On Holy Saturday, we remember your time in the tomb. Soon you will rise from the dead!

All: Dear Jesus, help us to love you more deeply.

Leader: At the Easter Vigil, we remember your Resurrection from the dead, the hope of our salvation!

All: Dear Jesus, help us to love you more deeply.

Activity

Write 1, 2, and 3 to put the Triduum events in the correct order.

☐ Jesus is in the tomb.

☐ Jesus washes the feet of his disciples.

☐ Jesus dies on the Cross.

Three especially sacred days help us remember that Jesus saved us.

Every spring, the Church celebrates three days called the Triduum. The Triduum is the high point of the whole Church year.

We remember the Last Supper in a special way on Holy Thursday. On Good Friday, we recall Jesus' Death on the Cross.

Starting at the Easter Vigil and on Easter Sunday, we remember that God raised Jesus from the dead. The Cross and the Resurrection are the greatest signs of God's love.

Jesus is the Savior of the world. He shares his risen life with us through the sacraments. During the Triduum, we remember and celebrate all these things in a special way.

Triduum

Did You Know?

 Jesus has many names.

Activity

Two names we have for Jesus are the Lamb of God and Savior of the World. With a partner, think of another name for Jesus.

Jesus is the _____.

Talk with your group about the name you gave Jesus.

Readers Theater

The Last Supper

Luke 22:7–20

Roles: Narrator 1, Narrator 2, Peter, Jesus, John

Jesus eats the Passover meal with the Apostles.

Narrator 1: The Apostles and Jesus were in Jerusalem.

Narrator 2: They were there to celebrate the Feast of Passover.

Narrator 1: Jesus asked Peter and John to find a room.

Narrator 2: They would all eat the Passover meal in that room.

Peter: Where should we look for a room?

Jesus: Go into the city. There, a man who carries a jar of water will meet you. He will show you the room.

John: We will go to look for this man. We will find a room.

Narrator 1: The disciples found the man with the water jar. This man took them to a large room.

Narrator 2: Peter and John made the room ready for the Passover meal.

Jesus: It is time for the Passover meal. I am happy to be here with you.

Narrator 1: Jesus took a cup. He blessed it and gave it to his Apostles.

Jesus: "Take this and share it among yourselves" (Luke 22:17). This is my blood.

Narrator 2: Then Jesus took bread. He blessed it, broke it, and gave it to his Apostles.

Jesus: I give you this bread to eat. "This is my body . . . do this in memory of me" (Luke 22:19).

Narrator 1: The Apostles shared the bread and wine with Jesus.

Narrator 2: Jesus asked them to share bread and wine with other people. This is how they would remember Jesus.

Why did Jesus die on the Cross and rise again?

Mini-Task

The Triduum is a time to remember that Jesus loved us so much that he died for us. Red and white are the colors of the Triduum. During the Triduum, we learn that Jesus washed the disciples' feet and that he died on the Cross. We remember how he followed God's plan, no matter what.

Design an icon for the Triduum. Choose colors and a picture for your icon.

Share your icon with a friend. Explain why you designed it to look the way it does.

Compare your symbol to other symbols you have designed for the Church year.

Triduum

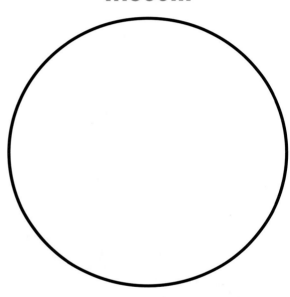

 Want to do more? Go to your Portfolio to continue this activity.

At Home

Talk about special meals you have shared as a family. What might it be like if Jesus were to join you for a meal? Welcome him in a Grace Before Meals prayer.

Copyright © by William H. Sadlier, Inc. All rights reserved.

How is the Risen Jesus present in his Church?

Easter

"He is not here, but he has been raised."

Luke 24:6

 **Prayer**

Gathering Prayer

Leader: Alleluia, Christ is risen.

All: Alleluia, Christ is risen.

Leader: This is the day that the Lord has made! Let us be glad and rejoice.

All: Alleluia, Christ is risen.

Leader: Jesus is alive! He has conquered sin and death.

All: Alleluia, Christ is risen.

Leader: Jesus promised his disciples that he would be raised from the dead.

All: Alleluia, Christ is risen.

Leader: Jesus died for us, but now he lives forever in heaven with God the Father.

All: Alleluia, Christ is risen.

Leader: Risen Jesus, we are filled with joy and your love for us!

All: Alleluia, Christ is risen.

Activity

Play a game of Guess Who with your friends. Give friends clues, and ask them to guess who you are describing. Use clues like this:

He died and in three days rose from the dead. Who is he?

Jesus brings new life at Easter.

Some of the women who were followers of Jesus visited his tomb on the morning of Easter Sunday. They found that the tomb was empty. An angel appeared and told them that Jesus was risen!

The women told others that Jesus was risen. The Apostles Peter and John ran as fast as they could to the tomb to see for themselves.

The Apostles saw the empty tomb. They began to believe that Jesus had risen from the dead, just as the angel said.

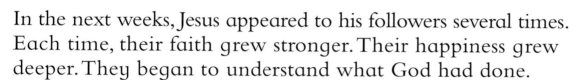

Easter

In the next weeks, Jesus appeared to his followers several times. Each time, their faith grew stronger. Their happiness grew deeper. They began to understand what God had done.

We speak of these events during the Easter season. Easter is a season of faith and joy as we come to understand that the Father raised the Son from the dead.

Did You Know?

 The Good News is announced in different ways.

Activity

Eggs are a symbol of new life. We sometimes decorate eggs at Easter to remind us of the new life Jesus gives us. Decorate the Easter egg with some signs and symbols of Easter!

Show your Easter egg to the rest of the group.

Easter Prayer Ritual

 "Over My Head," Tom Kendzia/OCP

Leader: During the season of Easter, we remember our Baptism. We will have holy water sprinkled on us at the beginning of Mass. We may see people being baptized when we go to Mass. We were baptized in the "living waters" of Christ and now live in the light of Christ.

As we come forward to bless ourselves in the waters of life, let us remember what it means to be washed in "living waters."

Leader: At our Baptism, we are anointed with holy oil and claimed as Christ's own.

All: We are washed in living water.

Leader: As we make the Sign of the Cross, let us remember the Cross of Jesus.

All: We are washed in living water.

Leader: We remember that we walk in the light of the Risen Christ.

All: We are washed in living water.

Leader: This water gives us new life, alleluia.

All: We are washed in living water.

Leader: In your goodness, O Lord, have mercy on us.

All: We are washed in living water.

Leader: In your compassion, O Lord, wipe out our sins.

All: We are washed in living water.

Leader: In your kindness, O Lord, wash away our fears.

All: We are washed in living water.

Leader: In your love, O God, create a clean heart in me.

All: We are washed in living water.

Leader: Living water, fill us with peace.

All: We are washed in living water.

Leader: Living water, fill us with hope,

All: We are washed in living water.

Leader: Wash us clean, as clean as new snow.

All: We are washed in living water.

(*After the blessing with water*)

Leader: Let us offer each other a sign of peace.

How is the Risen Jesus present in his Church?

Mini-Task

Easter is a time to celebrate that Jesus has risen to new life. White and gold are the colors of Easter.

During the Easter season, we hear the accounts of Jesus' followers who went to the empty tomb. We can imagine how amazed Jesus' followers must have been! We celebrate with joy.

Design an icon for Easter. Choose colors and a picture for your icon.

Share your icon with a friend. Can he or she guess which season it symbolizes? Explain why you designed it to look the way it does.

Compare your symbol to other symbols you have designed for the Church year.

Easter

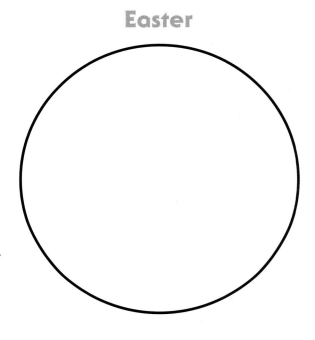

 Want to do more? Go to your Portfolio to continue this activity.

At Home

Before your evening meal or before bedtime, have your family members wash their hands and pray a few lines from the Prayer Ritual on pages 220–221.

Copyright © by William H. Sadlier, Inc. All rights reserved.

Who is the Holy Spirit?

Pentecost

"Come, Holy Spirit, fill the hearts of your faithful and kindle in them the fire of your love." *Roman Missal*

 **Prayer**

Gathering Prayer

Leader: Come, Holy Spirit, fill us with the gift of peace. We pray: Come, Holy Spirit.

All: Come, Holy Spirit.

Leader: Come, Holy Spirit, fill us with the gift of faith.

All: Come, Holy Spirit.

Leader: Come, Holy Spirit, fill us with the gift of hope.

All: Come, Holy Spirit.

Leader: Come, Holy Spirit, fill us with the gift of love.

All: Come, Holy Spirit.

Leader: Come, Holy Spirit, may we come to know you well.

All: Come, Holy Spirit.

Leader: Come, Holy Spirit, let us be a sign of hope for the world.

All: Come, Holy Spirit.

Leader: Come, Holy Spirit, let us share the gift of love with others.

All: Come, Holy Spirit.

Activity

List a gift you have asked for in the prayer above that you will try to live out this week.

The Holy Spirit came to Mary and the Apostles on Pentecost.

The last day of Easter is called Pentecost. It is a joyful celebration. The church is decorated in red, and we pray: "Come, Holy Spirit!"

After the Resurrection, the Risen Jesus told his followers to be the messengers of his peace and forgiveness. This was part of God's plan. God's people, the Church, continue to receive the Holy Spirit today so that they can carry on the mission of Jesus.

The Paschal candle is a symbol of the Risen Christ. At the end of the celebration of Pentecost, the Paschal candle is placed near the baptismal font for the rest of the year.

Does this mean that the mission of the Risen Jesus is finished? Not at all. Jesus continues his mission by sending the Holy Spirit upon the Church at Pentecost. The Holy Spirit makes present the mystery of Jesus most fully in the Eucharist.

Did You Know?

 Not all Paschal candles are the same.

Activity

Be a messenger of Jesus! Write one of the messages below on a piece of paper. Fold the paper however you like. Deliver your message about Jesus to a friend in your class. Read aloud the message a friend gives to you.

Jesus loves us.   Jesus forgives us.   Jesus brings us peace.

Pentecost Prayer Ritual

 "Go Out, Go Out," Curtis Stephan/OCP

Leader: In the name of the Father, and of the Son, and of the Holy Spirit, Amen.

Let us listen to what happened on the first Pentecost.

Jesus' closest followers were together. Suddenly, a noise like a strong wind came from the sky! Tongues of fire appeared. The disciples were filled with the Holy Spirit! They began to speak in different languages. They could proclaim the Good News of Jesus.

All: We proclaim your Good News, O Lord.

Leader: We are one in the Spirit. Make us one with you.

All: Holy Spirit, make us one with you.

Leader: Our hearts are filled with the fire of your love. Make us one with you.

All: Holy Spirit, make us one with you.

Leader: Spirit of the living God, wash over us. Make us one with you.

All: Holy Spirit, make us one with you.

Leader: You have anointed us, O God, with your Holy Spirit. Make us one with you.

All: Holy Spirit, make us one with you.

Leader: The Spirit of the Lord has filled the whole world, alleluia.

All: Holy Spirit, make us one with you.

Leader: Come forward and be signed with the Sign of the Cross. Let us pray.

Lord, by the light of the Holy Spirit
you have taught the hearts of your faithful.
In the same Spirit help us to do and love what
is right and always be joyful in your mercy.
We ask this through Christ our Lord.

All: Amen.

Who is the Holy Spirit?

Mini-Task

Pentecost is a time to celebrate that the Holy Spirit brought strength to the Apostles after Jesus returned to his Father in heaven.

Red is the color of Pentecost. Red reminds us of the fire of the Holy Spirit. The Holy Spirit helped the Apostles spread the word about Jesus. We celebrate that we have the same mission as the Apostles did—to tell the world about Jesus!

Pentecost

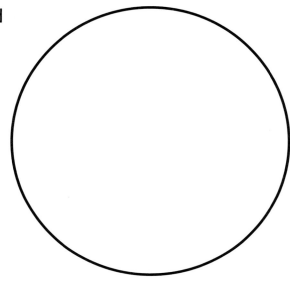

Design an icon for Pentecost. Choose colors and a picture for your icon.

Share your icon with a friend. Can he or she guess which season it symbolizes? Explain why you designed it to look the way it does.

 Want to do more? Go to your Portfolio to continue this activity.

 At Home

The Holy Spirit helped the disciples speak in different languages. Does anyone in your family know any words in another language that describe Jesus?

Copyright © by William H. Sadlier, Inc. All rights reserved.

How do we grow as Jesus' followers?

Ordinary Time

"Your Father is pleased to give you the kingdom." Luke 12:32

 **Prayer**

Gathering Prayer

Leader: Ordinary Time makes up the longest season of the Church year. During this time, we learn about Jesus' work and travels. We hear of his miracles, and we listen to his parables. We learn especially about how we should love God and each other.

Jesus, teach us your ways.

All: Jesus, teach us your ways.

Leader: You cured the man who could not speak. May we tell of your great love for us.

All: Jesus, teach us your ways.

Leader: Help us, Lord, to love one another as you have loved us.

All: Jesus, teach us your ways.

Leader: Jesus, help us to always celebrate your love in us.

All: Jesus, teach us your ways.

Activity

Draw one thing that Jesus has taught you. Explain your drawing to a friend.

Jesus shows us the way to the Kingdom of God.

During the season of Ordinary Time, the Church remembers all the wonderful things Jesus taught and did. We remember how he loved everyone.

Jesus especially loved children. He said: "Let the children come to me" (Matthew 19:14). He taught children that they could enter the Kingdom of God by following him.

During Ordinary Time, we also remember how Jesus takes care of us. He is like a shepherd, and we are his flock. He cares for each one of his sheep.

He protects us from danger and will not let any harm come to us. We are always happy when we are with Jesus.

The color of Ordinary Time is green. Green reminds us of growing things. Ordinary Time is a season to rejoice because Jesus cares for us.

Did You Know?

 We never grow alone.

Activity

Circle the ways you can grow in faith during Ordinary Time.

pray   read the Bible   **play**

go to Mass   **watch movies**

Readers Theater

Blessed Are You

Matthew 5:1–12

Roles: Narrator 1, Narrator 2, Readers 1–10

The Beatitudes offer Jesus' disciples a new way to live.

Narrator 1: A big crowd of people had come to see Jesus.

Narrator 2: Many of them were sick. Jesus cured them all.

Narrator 1: Jesus found a place to sit.

Narrator 2: There he began to teach the people.

Reader 1: "Blessed are the poor in spirit,
for theirs is the kingdom of heaven" (Matthew 5:3).

Reader 2: "Blessed are they who mourn,
for they will be comforted" (Matthew 5:4).

Reader 3: "Blessed are the meek,
for they will inherit the land" (Matthew 5:5).

Reader 4: "Blessed are they who hunger and thirst for
righteousness,
for they will be satisfied" (Matthew 5:6).

Reader 5: "Blessed are the merciful,
for they will be shown mercy" (Matthew 5:7).

Reader 6: "Blessed are the clean of heart,
for they will see God" (Matthew 5:8).

Reader 7: "Blessed are the peacemakers,
for they will be called children of God" (Matthew 5:9).

Reader 8: "Blessed are they who are persecuted for the sake of righteousness,
for theirs is the kingdom of heaven" (Matthew 5:10).

Reader 9: "Blessed are you when they insult you and persecute you and utter every kind of evil against you [falsely] because of me" (Matthew 5:11).

Reader 10: "Rejoice and be glad, for your reward will be great in heaven" (Matthew 5:12).

Narrator 1: Jesus gave his disciples a new way to live.

Narrator 2: It is a way of love and peace!

How do we grow as Jesus' followers?

Mini-Task

In Ordinary Time, we remember all the wonderful things Jesus taught. We remember how Jesus takes care of us.

He taught children that they could enter the Kingdom of God by following him. Ordinary Time is a season to rejoice because Jesus cares for us.

Ordinary Time

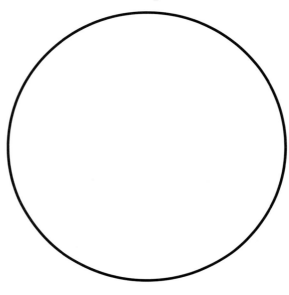

Green is the color of Ordinary Time. The church is decorated in a simpler way than at feast days like Christmas and Easter.

Design an icon for Ordinary Time. Choose colors and a picture for your icon. Share your icon with a friend. Can he or she guess which season it symbolizes? Explain why you designed it to look the way it does.

 Want to do more? Go to your Portfolio to continue this activity.

At Home

Talk together about how family members have grown. Look at baby pictures and share stories of your childhood. Talk about how your faith has grown, too.

Copyright © by William H. Sadlier, Inc. All rights reserved.

Welcome

to your *Christ In Us* Sourcebook

Sign of the Cross

In the name of the Father,
and of the Son,
and of the Holy Spirit.
Amen.

Our Father

Our Father, who art in heaven,
hallowed be thy name;
thy kingdom come,
thy will be done on earth as it
    is in heaven.
Give us this day our daily bread;
and forgive us our trespasses
as we forgive those who
    trespass against us;
and lead us not into temptation,
but deliver us from evil.
Amen.

Hail Mary

Hail Mary, full of grace,
the Lord is with you!
Blessed are you among women,
and blessed is the fruit of
    your womb, Jesus.
Holy Mary, Mother of God,
pray for us sinners,
now and at the hour of our death.
Amen.

Glory Be to the Father

Glory be to the Father
and to the Son
and to the Holy Spirit,
as it was in the beginning
is now, and ever shall be
world without end.
Amen.

Apostles' Creed

I believe in God, the Father almighty,
   Creator of heaven and earth,
and in Jesus Christ, his only Son,
   our Lord,
who was conceived by the Holy
   Spirit,
born of the Virgin Mary,
suffered under Pontius Pilate,
was crucified, died and was buried;
he descended into hell;
on the third day he rose again
from the dead;
he ascended into heaven,
and is seated at the right hand
   of God the Father almighty;
from there he will come to judge
   the living and the dead.
I believe in the Holy Spirit,
   the holy Catholic Church,
   the communion of saints,
   the forgiveness of sins,
   the resurrection of the body,
   and life everlasting. Amen.

Act of Contrition

My God,
I am sorry for my sins with
   all my heart.
In choosing to do wrong
and failing to do good,
I have sinned against you
whom I should love above
   all things.
I firmly intend, with your help,
to do penance,
to sin no more,
and to avoid whatever
   leads me to sin.
Our Savior Jesus Christ
suffered and died for us.
In his name, my God, have mercy.
Amen.

Grace Before Meals

Bless us, O Lord,
    and these your gifts
which we are about to receive
from your goodness.
Through Christ our Lord.
Amen.

Grace After Meals

We give you thanks, almighty God,
for these and all your gifts,
which we have received through
Christ our Lord.
Amen.

Angel of God

Angel of God,
my guardian dear,
to whom God's love
    commits me here,
ever this day be at my side,
to light and guard, to rule
    and guide.
Amen.

The Rosary

A rosary is made up of groups of beads arranged in a circle. It begins with a cross, followed by one large bead and three small ones. The next large bead (just before the medal) begins the first "decade." Each decade consists of one large bead followed by ten smaller beads.

Begin to pray the Rosary with the Sign of the Cross. Recite the Apostles' Creed. Then pray one Our Father, three Hail Marys, and one Glory Be to the Father.

To pray each decade, say an Our Father on the large bead and a Hail Mary on each of the ten smaller beads. Close each decade by praying the Glory Be to the Father. Pray the Hail, Holy Queen as the last prayer of the Rosary.

The mysteries of the Rosary are special events in the lives of Jesus and Mary. As you pray each decade, think of the appropriate Joyful Mystery, Sorrowful Mystery, Glorious Mystery, or Mystery of Light.

The Five Joyful Mysteries

1. The Annunciation
2. The Visitation
3. The Birth of Jesus
4. The Presentation of Jesus in the Temple
5. The Finding of Jesus in the Temple

The Five Sorrowful Mysteries

1. The Agony in the Garden
2. The Scourging at the Pillar
3. The Crowning with Thorns
4. The Carrying of the Cross
5. The Crucifixion and Death of Jesus

The Five Glorious Mysteries

1. The Resurrection
2. The Ascension
3. The Descent of the Holy Spirit upon the Apostles
4. The Assumption of Mary into Heaven
5. The Coronation of Mary as Queen of Heaven

The Five Mysteries of Light

1. Jesus' Baptism in the Jordan
2. The Miracle at the Wedding at Cana
3. Jesus Announces the Kingdom of God
4. The Transfiguration
5. The Institution of the Eucharist

The Ten Commandments

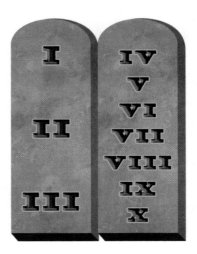

1. I am the LORD your God: you shall not have strange gods before me.
2. You shall not take the name of the LORD your God in vain.
3. Remember to keep holy the LORD's Day.
4. Honor your father and your mother.
5. You shall not kill.
6. You shall not commit adultery.
7. You shall not steal.
8. You shall not bear false witness against your neighbor.
9. You shall not covet your neighbor's wife.
10. You shall not covet your neighbor's goods.

The Seven Sacraments

Baptism
Eucharist
Penance and Reconciliation
Confirmation
Matrimony
Holy Orders
Anointing of the Sick

Stations of the Cross

In the Stations of the Cross, we follow in the footsteps of Jesus during his Passion and Death on the Cross.

1 Jesus is condemned to die.

2 Jesus takes up his cross.

3 Jesus falls the first time.

4 Jesus meets his mother.

5 Simon helps Jesus carry his cross.

6 Veronica wipes the face of Jesus.

7 Jesus falls the second time.

8 Jesus meets the women of Jerusalem.

9 Jesus falls the third time.

10 Jesus is stripped of his garments.

11 Jesus is nailed to the Cross.

12 Jesus dies on the Cross.

13 Jesus is taken down from the Cross.

14 Jesus is laid in the tomb.

The Beatitudes

✜ "Blessed are the poor in spirit,
    for theirs is the kingdom
      of heaven.

✜ Blessed are they who mourn,
    for they will be comforted.

✜ Blessed are the meek,
    for they will inherit the land.

✜ Blessed are they who hunger
    and thirst for righteousness,
      for they will be satisfied.

✜ Blessed are the merciful,
    for they will be shown mercy.

✜ Blessed are the clean of heart,
    for they will see God.

✜ Blessed are the peacemakers,
    for they will be called children
      of God.

✜ Blessed are they who are persecuted
    for the sake of righteousness,
      for theirs is the kingdom of heaven."

(Matthew 5:3–10)

Your *Christ In Us*

Family Companion

Welcome. We are so glad that you are a ***Christ In Us*** family. In this section, you will find a treasury of resources as your family accompanies your child on our journey to a greater love in Jesus Christ. This material is written specifically for you as adult family members. But be certain that you review your child's resources that precede this section. Also, don't forget to look over the *Glossary* that follows. It will give you a good overview of what your child has been experiencing this year. Finally, the *Q&A* offers a wonderful opportunity for your entire family to review the major faith statements of the grade.

Book

Chapter

Verse

Passage

Passage Title

Titles are sometimes added to show themes of the chapters, but these titles are not part of the actual words of the Bible.

Praise of the Father |21| *t u**At that very moment he rejoiced [in] the holy Spirit and said, "I give you praise, Father, Lord of heaven and earth, for although you have hidden these things from the wise and the learned you have revealed them to the childlike. Yes, Father, such has been your gracious will. 22 *v*All things have been handed over to me by my Father. No one knows who the Son is except the Father, and who the Father is except the Son and anyone to whom the Son wishes to reveal him."

A passage is a section of a chapter made up of a number of verses.

This passage shows Luke 10:21–22, which means: the Gospel of Luke, chapter ten, verses twenty-one to twenty-two.

Reading the Bible . . . in Five Easy Steps

When you are given a Scripture passage to read, here are five easy steps that will help you to find it! With your child, follow these steps to look up **Lk 10:21–22**.

1. **Find the book.** When the name of the book is abbreviated, locate the meaning of the abbreviation on the contents pages at the beginning of your Bible. *Lk* stands for Luke, one of the four Gospels.

2. **Find the page.** Your Bible's contents pages will also show the page on which the book begins. Turn to that page within your Bible.

3. **Find the chapter.** Once you arrive at the page where the book begins, keep turning the pages forward until you find the right chapter. The image above shows you how a chapter number is usually displayed on a typical Bible page. You are looking for chapter **10** in Luke.

4. **Find the verses.** Once you find the right chapter, locate the verse or verses you need within the chapter. The image above also shows you how verse numbers will look on a typical Bible page. You are looking for verses **21** and **22**.

5. **Start reading!**

Visits to the Blessed Sacrament

Before Mass on Sundays or at other special times, take a few minutes to visit Jesus, present in the Blessed Sacrament. After you have taken your place in church, kneel or sit quietly. Be very still. Talk to Jesus about your needs and your hopes. Thank Jesus for his great love. Remember to pray for your family and your parish, especially anyone who is sick or in need.

Prayer Before the Blessed Sacrament

Jesus,
You are God-with-us,
especially in this sacrament
of the Eucharist.
You love me as I am
and help me grow.

Come and be with me
in all my joys and sorrows.
Help me share your peace and love
with everyone I meet.
I ask in your name.
Amen.

Holy Days of Obligation

Each Sunday of the liturgical year is a great celebration of the Church, or a solemnity. In addition to each Sunday, the Church has other solemnities in the liturgical year on which we are obliged to attend Mass to give special honor to Jesus Christ for the salvation he has given to us. These are called Holy Days of Obligation. Post this list of holy days in your home to remind everyone of them!

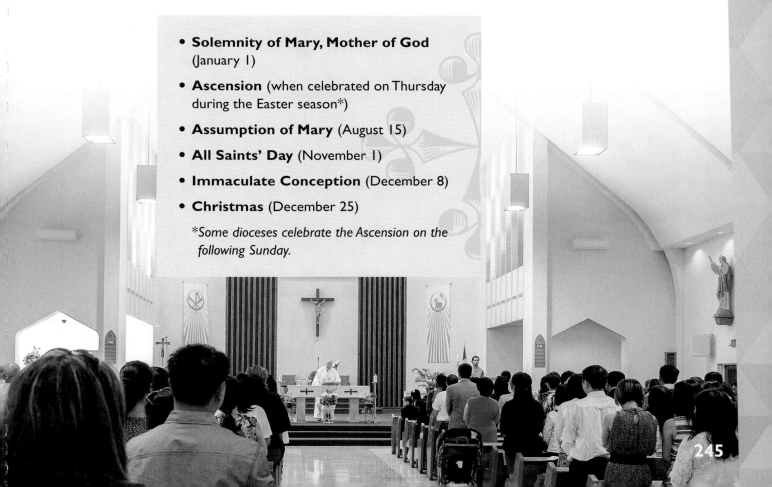

- **Solemnity of Mary, Mother of God** (January 1)

- **Ascension** (when celebrated on Thursday during the Easter season*)

- **Assumption of Mary** (August 15)

- **All Saints' Day** (November 1)

- **Immaculate Conception** (December 8)

- **Christmas** (December 25)

  *Some dioceses celebrate the Ascension on the following Sunday.

Catholic Beliefs

Everlasting Life

Through his suffering, Death, and Resurrection, Jesus brought us from death to life, from despair to the fulfillment of our deepest hope—everlasting life. Just as we believe in Jesus' Resurrection, we have hope in our own resurrection and eternal happiness with God after we die. Point out this belief when you pray the Nicene Creed as a family.

Nicene Creed

I believe in one God,
   the Father almighty,
   maker of heaven and earth,
   of all things visible and invisible.

I believe in one Lord Jesus Christ,
   the Only Begotten Son of God,
   born of the Father before all ages.
   God from God, Light from Light,
   true God from true God,
   begotten, not made, consubstantial
      with the Father;
   through him all things were made.
   For us men and for our salvation
      he came down from heaven,
   and by the Holy Spirit
      was incarnate of the Virgin Mary,
         and became man.

For our sake he was crucified
      under Pontius Pilate,
   he suffered death and was buried,
   and rose again on the third day
      in accordance with the Scriptures.
   He ascended into heaven
      and is seated at the right hand
         of the Father.
   He will come again in glory to judge
      the living and the dead
      and his kingdom will have no end.

I believe in the Holy Spirit, the Lord,
      the giver of life,
   who proceeds from the Father and the Son,
   who with the Father and the Son is
      adored and glorified,
   who has spoken through the prophets.

I believe in one, holy, catholic
      and apostolic Church.
   I confess one Baptism for the
      forgiveness of sins
   and I look forward to the resurrection of the dead
      and the life of the world to come.
Amen.

Your *Christ In Us*
Sacramental Preparation Companion

The following pages will help prepare you to receive the Sacrament of Penance and Reconciliation and the Sacrament of the Eucharist. This is a time of great joy! Your friends and the parish community are praying for you.

Examination of Conscience

In the Bible, Jesus tells us a story about a father and two sons: the younger son made a choice to leave his family. He wanted to spend a lot of money on foolish things. After the son spent all his money, he had nowhere to go. He thought about the foolish choice he had made. He realized that his choices were unloving to God and his family. (see Luke 15:11–32, **The Prodigal Son**)

We should think about whether our choices show love for God, others, and ourselves. When we do this, we make an **examination of conscience**. To help prepare to celebrate the Sacrament of Penance and Reconciliation, we learn to make an examination of conscience.

When we make an examination of conscience, we follow these steps:

We ask the Holy Spirit to help us to remember the choices we have made.

We think about the ways we have or have not followed and obeyed the Ten Commandments. (See page 240 to read the Ten Commandments.)

Remember that God loves you and forgives you.

Examination of Conscience continued

We ask ourselves if we have hurt others on purpose.

We ask ourselves if there were times we could have done something good for others but did not.

Here are some questions you can ask when you examine your conscience:

Reverence for God:

Did I take the time to pray?

Do I go to Mass on Sundays and other Holy Days?

Did I speak God's name only with honor and praise?

Respect for Myself:

Did I take care of my body?

Did I give thanks for my family, friends, and all who love me?

Respect for Others:

Did I obey my parents and all those who take care of me?

Did I hurt other people by what I said or did?

Did I act with honesty?

Did I look for ways to help others?

Follow the steps and questions you learned to make an examination of conscience.

How to Receive the Sacrament of Penance and Reconciliation

Here is what happens when you celebrate the Sacrament of Penance in **individual confession**.

The priest welcomes you, and you both make the Sign of the Cross. You listen as the priest reads from Scripture about God's forgiveness.

You confess your sins to the priest. You and the priest talk about making right choices. The priest gives you an act of penance. You will do your penance after the celebration of the sacrament.

You pray an Act of Contrition. You tell God you are sorry for your sins and that you will try not to sin again. The priest prays the words of absolution, stretching his right hand over your head. In God's name, your sins are forgiven by the priest.

You and the priest praise and thank God for his love and forgiveness. The priest tells you: "The Lord has freed you from your sins. Go in peace."

We can celebrate the sacrament in a **communal celebration with individual confession.** This is what we do.

We gather and sing a hymn together. Then the priest welcomes us. We listen to readings from Scripture about God's love and forgiveness.

The priest talks to us about the readings. We listen to questions that are part of an examination of conscience.

We pray an Act of Contrition together. We pray the Lord's Prayer. Each penitent privately tells his or her sins to the priest. The priest tells each penitent to do an act of penance. The priest stretches his right hand over each penitent's head and prays the words of absolution.

Together we all praise and thank God for his mercy. The priest blesses the parish community. He tells all of us: "The Lord has freed you from your sins. Go in peace."

The Mass: The Celebration of the Eucharist

Every Sunday we gather with our parish to worship God as our Creator and Lord. We do this in the greatest prayer of thanksgiving, which we call the Eucharist. The celebration of the Eucharist is also called the **Mass**. By special words and actions, we show that we believe that God is with us. Most of all, we remember and celebrate how Jesus saved us by his suffering, Death, Resurrection, and Ascension. The community of people who gather for the celebration of the Eucharist is called the **assembly**. Our parish priest leads the assembly in this celebration. He is called the celebrant. A deacon often assists him. At Mass the priest and the deacon wear special clothing called **vestments**.

It was on a Sunday that Jesus Christ rose from the dead to new life. So, Sunday is the most special day for the Church. Sunday is called the **Lord's Day**. Its celebration lasts from Saturday evening through Sunday until midnight. We gather with our parish to celebrate the Mass on this day because it is the day Jesus rose from the dead. We celebrate the salvation that Jesus made possible by his sacrifice on the Cross. He fills us, the Body of Christ, with the grace of his salvation. The celebration of the Eucharist is the center of the Church's life. On Sunday we also rest from work and take time to be with our family.

We worship God by taking part in the Mass every Sunday of the year. We are also to attend Mass on other special days called Holy Days of Obligation. When we do this, we follow the Third Commandment and one of the laws of the Church.

1. **sanctuary** the part of the church that includes the altar and the ambo. The word *sanctuary* means "holy place."

2. **altar** the special table that is the center of the celebration of the Liturgy of the Eucharist, also called the Table of the Lord

3. **crucifix** a cross with a figure of Christ crucified, displayed in the sanctuary

4. **tabernacle** the special place in the church in which the Most Blessed Sacrament is placed in reserve

5. **sanctuary lamp** light or candle that is always lit near the tabernacle. It helps us to remember that Jesus is really present in the Most Blessed Sacrament.

6. **ambo** a sacred reading stand called the Table of the Word of God. The ambo is used only for proclamation of the Scripture in the liturgy.

7. **chalice** the special cup into which the priest pours grape wine that becomes the Blood of Christ during the Liturgy of the Eucharist

8. **paten** the special plate on which the priest places the wheat bread that becomes the Body of Christ during the Liturgy of the Eucharist

9. **cruets** small glass jars that contain the water and the grape wine used at Mass

10. **presider's chair** chair on which the priest who is celebrating Mass sits

11 processional cross cross with a figure of Christ crucified that is carried in the entrance procession and may also be carried during the Offertory procession and during the recessional

12 Paschal candle a large candle that is blessed and lit every Easter. It represents the Risen Christ among us. The flame of the Paschal candle is used to light baptismal candles.

13 baptismal font or pool contains the water that is blessed and used during the Sacrament of Baptism

14 Stations of the Cross fourteen pictures that help us to follow the footsteps of Jesus during his Passion and Death on the Cross

15 Reconciliation Room or confessional a separate space for celebrating the Sacrament of Penance and Reconciliation. This is where you meet the priest for individual confession and absolution. You may sit and talk to him face-to-face or kneel behind a screen.

16 stained glass colorful windows that may show saints or scenes from Scripture

17 pews where the assembly is seated during the celebration of Mass

18 statue of Mary image of the Mother of God, our greatest saint. Statues of other saints may also be found in the church.

Introductory Rites

The Mass begins with the **Introductory Rites**. These prayers and actions help us to remember that we are a worshiping community. They prepare us to listen to the Word of God and celebrate the Eucharist.

In the Introductory Rites, we stand and sing to express our unity as the baptized. As the assembly sings, the priest, deacon, and other ministers process to the altar.

Those in the procession bow to the altar or genuflect to the tabernacle, and the priest and deacon kiss the altar as a sign of reverence for the Lord's Table.

We make the Sign of the Cross. Then the priest greets us. His words and our response remind us that we gather in God's name.

The priest asks us to silently think about our sins, the times we have not loved God and others.

Together with the priest we praise God for his love and forgiveness. We may pray:

"Lord, have mercy."
"Christ, have mercy."
"Lord, have mercy."

We often sing or say a prayer of praise to God the Father, God the Son, and God the Holy Spirit. This prayer begins with the words:

"Glory to God in the highest,
and on earth peace to people
of good will."

The priest prays an opening prayer to remind us we are in God's presence. We respond: "Amen."

The Liturgy of the Word

The **Liturgy of the Word** is the part of the Mass in which we listen to Scripture being proclaimed. To *proclaim* means "to announce."

On most Sundays the first reading is from the Old Testament. From this reading we learn what God did for the Jewish People before Jesus was born. We learn that God's love for his people never ends. The Responsorial Psalm is our response to the first reading. A cantor sings or a reader proclaims the psalm. We sing or say a response.

The second reading is from the New Testament. During this reading we listen to the teachings of the Apostles and other disciples.

A reader, or **lector**, reads the first two readings. They are read from a book called the **Lectionary**. The lector stands at the ambo to read. An **ambo** is a sacred reading stand, the Table of the Word of God. We sit and listen to the readings.

The third reading is the **Gospel**. On most Sundays we sing *Alleluia* before the Gospel is read. When we listen to the Gospel, we learn the Good News about Jesus Christ and how to live as his disciples.

A priest or deacon stands at the ambo to read from the Gospel of Matthew, Mark, Luke, or John. The Gospel is most often read from a special book called the **Book of the Gospels**. We stand as the Gospel is read because the Gospel has a place of honor in the Liturgy of the Word.

Throughout the year, as the Church proclaims the readings at Mass, we remember and celebrate the whole mystery of Christ. We celebrate the Incarnation, or the Son of God becoming man, and the Nativity, or the birth of Jesus. We celebrate Jesus' Death, Resurrection, and Ascension, his sending of the Holy Spirit on Pentecost, and his coming again at the end of time.

Responding to the Word of God

After we have heard all the readings, the priest or deacon talks to us about them. This talk is called the **homily**. When we listen carefully to the homily, we learn more about God. We learn ways we can share God's love with others. When the homily is finished, we pray the **Creed**. In the Creed we proclaim the faith of the Church.

After the Creed we pray the **Prayer of the Faithful**. In the Prayer of the Faithful, we pray for the needs of the Church. We pray for the pope, other Church leaders, and all God's people. We pray for world leaders. We pray for people throughout the world, especially for those who are sick or in need. We pray for the people in our parish who have died. We pray for people in our lives who need God's love and help. We ask God to hear our prayer.

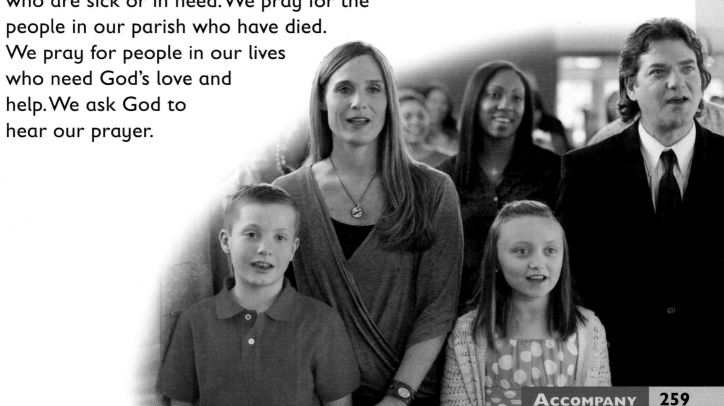

The Liturgy of the Eucharist

Jesus told his disciples to remember what he did at the Last Supper. He told them to celebrate this special meal again and again. He said: "Do this in memory of me" (Luke 22:19).

The word *eucharist* means "to give thanks." Throughout the Mass, we give thanks and praise to God. Like the disciples at the Last Supper, we gather around a table. This special table is called the **altar**. The altar is the focal point of the Liturgy of the Eucharist.

The **Liturgy of the Eucharist** is the part of the Mass in which the bread and wine become the Body and Blood of Jesus Christ. The Liturgy of the Eucharist begins as the priest prepares the altar. Very often members of the assembly bring forward the gifts of bread and wine. We remember the many gifts God has given to us. We offer these gifts and ourselves to God.

The Liturgy of the Eucharist has these parts:
- Preparation of the Gifts
- Prayer over the Offerings
- Eucharistic Prayer
- Communion Rite

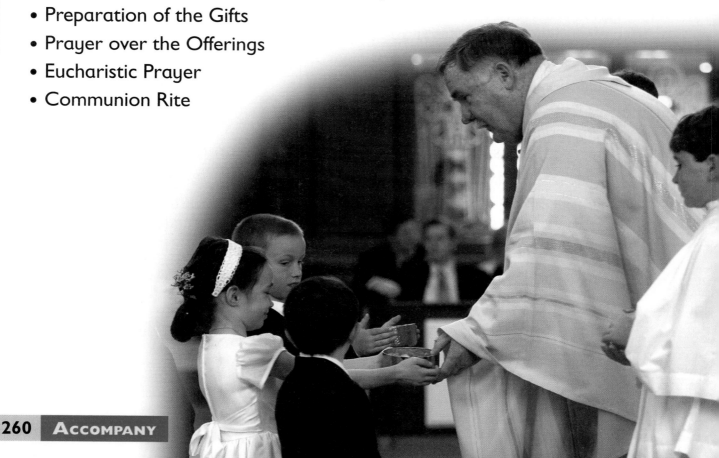

The priest or deacon accepts the gifts of bread and wine and places them on the altar. As he prepares the bread and wine, the priest prays special prayers. We respond: "Blessed be God for ever." Then we pray with the priest that the Lord will accept these gifts.

Throughout the Liturgy of the Eucharist, we remember that the Mass is a sacrifice. A **sacrifice** is an offering of a gift to God. When Jesus was on earth he offered his life for us on the Cross to save us from sin. He rose from the dead on Easter Sunday so that we could live peacefully with God forever. Jesus' work of salvation through his life, Death, and Resurrection is called his Passover. It is remembered and made present in every Mass. And it is Jesus Christ himself who acts through the priest and offers the Eucharistic sacrifice.

The Eucharistic Prayer

After the gifts are prepared, we pray the Eucharistic Prayer. The **Eucharistic Prayer** is the center of the Mass and the Church's greatest prayer of praise and thanksgiving.

The priest prays the Eucharistic Prayer in the name of the whole Church. He prays to God the Father through Jesus Christ in the Holy Spirit. Through the power of the Holy Spirit the priest says and does what Jesus said and did at the Last Supper. Taking the bread, the priest says:

> "Take this, all of you, and eat of it,
> for this is my Body,
> which will be given up for you."

Then taking the cup of wine he says:

> "Take this, all of you, and drink from it,
> for this is the chalice of my Blood...."

This part of the Eucharistic Prayer is called the **Consecration**.

During the Liturgy of the Eucharist the priest uses a special plate and cup. The plate is called a **paten**. The priest places the wheat bread that becomes the Body of Christ on the paten. The cup is called a **chalice**. The priest pours the grape wine that becomes the Blood of Christ into the chalice.

By the power of the Holy Spirit and through the words and actions of the priest, the bread and wine become the Body and Blood of Christ. In a way that we cannot fully understand, Jesus Christ is really present in the Eucharist. We call this the **Real Presence**. The changing of the bread and wine into the Body and Blood of Christ is called *transubstantiation*.

The priest invites us to proclaim our faith. We may pray:

"When we eat this Bread and drink this Cup, we proclaim your Death, O Lord, until you come again."

We pray that the Holy Spirit will unite all who believe in Jesus. We end the Eucharistic Prayer by praying "Amen." When we do this, we are saying "Yes, I believe." We are saying "yes" to the prayer the priest has prayed in our name.

Preparing for Holy Communion

In the Liturgy of the Eucharist, after the Eucharistic Prayer, we prepare to receive Jesus himself in the Eucharist. Through the power of the Holy Spirit and the action of the priest, our gifts of bread and wine have now become the Body and Blood of Christ. And we will receive the Body and Blood of Christ in **Holy Communion**. Like the disciples at Emmaus, we recognize Jesus "in the breaking of the bread."

We join ourselves with the whole Church as we pray aloud or sing the Lord's Prayer. Then the priest reminds us of Jesus' words at the Last Supper. Jesus said: "Peace I leave with you; my peace I give to you" (John 14:27). We pray that Christ's peace may be with us always. We share a sign of peace with the people who are near us. When we do this, we show that we are united to the Risen Lord, Jesus Christ, and to one another as the Body of Christ.

After we share a sign of peace, we pray to Jesus, who sacrificed his life to save us from sin. We ask him for forgiveness and peace. We begin the prayer with these words:

> "Lamb of God, you take away
> the sins of the world,
> have mercy on us."

As we pray the Lamb of God, the priest breaks the **Host**, the Bread that has become the Body of Christ. The priest puts a small piece in the chalice as a sign of the unity of the Body and Blood of Jesus Christ.

How to Receive Holy Communion

After we pray the Lamb of God, the priest invites us to receive Jesus Christ in Holy Communion. The priest prays:

"Behold the Lamb of God,
behold him who takes away the sins of the world.
Blessed are those called to the supper of the Lamb."

Together with the priest we pray:

"Lord, I am not worthy
that you should enter under my roof,
but only say the word
and my soul shall be healed."

Then we go forward with reverence and love to receive Jesus in Holy Communion. Each of us stands before the priest, deacon, or extraordinary minister of Holy Communion, who raises the Host before us. We bow our head. The priest, deacon, or extraordinary minister says: "The Body of Christ." We respond: "Amen" and then receive the Host in the hand or on the tongue.

If we are also receiving from the chalice, the priest, deacon, or extraordinary minister of Holy Communion raises the chalice. Again, we bow our head. The priest, deacon, or extraordinary minister says: "The Blood of Christ." We respond: "Amen" and then drink from the cup.

As the gathered assembly joins in procession and receives the Body and Blood of Christ, we sing a hymn to express our unity. We are united with the whole Church, the Body of Christ.

After everyone has received Holy Communion there is usually some time for quiet prayer. During this time we remember that Jesus is present within us. We thank Jesus for the gift of himself in Holy Communion.

Concluding Rites

Jesus sent his disciples out to continue his work. We are disciples of Jesus. He wants us to keep doing his work, too. He wants us to share God's love with others in our homes, schools, parishes, neighborhoods, cities or towns, and throughout the world. God's grace helps us to do all that he asks. We are reminded of this call at Mass.

The celebration of the Mass ends with the **Concluding Rites**. The priest gives us a **blessing**. This final blessing is a prayer asking God to keep us in his care. The priest blesses us with the Sign of the Cross as he says:

> "May almighty God bless you,
> the Father, and the Son, ✠
> and the Holy Spirit."

We respond: "Amen."

Then the priest or deacon dismisses us, or sends us out, as baptized members of the Church, to share God's love with others. He says one of the following:

- "Go in peace."
- "Go forth, the Mass is ended."
- "Go and announce the Gospel of the Lord."
- "Go in peace, glorifying the Lord by your life."

We respond: "Thanks be to God."

After the dismissal, sometimes we sing a hymn. The priest, deacon, and other ministers process out of the church. All through the week we remember Jesus' promise to be with us always.

What are some ways you can "go in peace, glorifying the Lord by your life"?

Works of Mercy

Jesus taught us that each person is a gift from God. We are to help people who are in need. **Works of Mercy** are things we can do to help care for the needs of others. There are Corporal Works of Mercy and Spiritual Works of Mercy. The Works of Mercy are meant to help people receive the things they need. For example, we all need food, water, and clothing. We also need a place to live. And when we are sick, we need caring people to help us feel better.

There are Works of Mercy that help people in other ways. We share God's peace when we are patient and forgiving. And with a smile or a kind word, we can comfort someone who is sad or lonely. Jesus also taught us to pray for the needs of others.

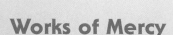

Works of Mercy

Corporal
Feed the hungry.
Give drink to the thirsty.
Clothe the naked.
Visit the imprisoned.
Shelter the homeless.
Visit the sick.
Bury the dead.

Spiritual
Admonish the sinner.
Instruct the ignorant.
Counsel the doubtful.
Comfort the sorrowful.
Bear wrongs patiently.
Forgive all injuries.
Pray for the living and the dead.

Sacramental Preparation at Home

Human dignity is the value and worth that come from being created in God's image and likeness. Jesus stood up for the human dignity of every person. Jesus taught us to show love for God, others, and ourselves.

The Seven Themes of Catholic Social Teaching

Jesus' life and teachings are the foundation of Catholic social teaching. Your child is preparing to receive First Holy Communion. Help your child become familiar with Catholic social teaching, which calls us to work for justice and peace as Jesus did. As a family, discuss ways in which you can work together for justice and peace.

1. **Life and Dignity of the Human Person** Human life is sacred because it is a gift from God. Because we are all God's children, we all share the same human dignity. As Christians, we respect all people, even those we do not know.

2. **Call to Family, Community, and Participation** We are all social. We need to be with others to grow. The family is the basic community. In the family, we grow and learn the values of our faith. As Christians, we live those values in our family and community.

3. **Rights and Responsibilities of the Human Person** Every person has a fundamental right to life. This includes the things we need to have a decent life: faith and family, work and education, health care and housing. We also have a responsibility to others and to society. We work to make sure the rights of all people are protected.

4. **Option for the Poor and Vulnerable** We have a special obligation to help those who are poor and in need. This includes those who cannot protect themselves because of their age or their health.

5. **Dignity of Work and the Rights of Workers** Our work is a sign of our participation in God's work. People have the right to decent work, just wages, safe working conditions, and participation in decisions about work.

6. **Solidarity of the Human Family** Solidarity is a feeling of unity. It binds together members of a group. Each of us is a member of the one human family. The human family includes people of all racial and cultural backgrounds. We all suffer when one part of the human family suffers, whether they live near or far away.

7. **Care for God's Creation** God created us to be stewards, or caretakers, of his creation. We must care for and respect the environment. We have to protect it for future generations. When we care for creation, we show respect for God the Creator.

Fold on this line.

Cut on this line.

My ✤ Mass Book

Concluding Rites

The priest blesses us. The priest or deacon may say: "Go in peace." We say: **"Thanks be to God."**

We stand and sing a gathering song. We pray the Sign of the Cross. The priest says: "The Lord be with you." We answer: **"And with your spirit."** We ask God and one another for forgiveness.

Introductory Rite

We gather with our parish to worship God. We remember and celebrate what Jesus said and did at the Last Supper.

Fold on this line.

We praise God as we sing or say: **"Glory to God in the highest, and on earth peace to people of good will."**

We go out to live as Jesus' followers.

Then the priest invites us to share in the Eucharist. As people receive the Body and Blood of Christ, they answer: **"Amen."** While this is happening, we sing a song of thanks.

We get ready to receive Jesus. Together we pray or sing the Our Father. Then we share a sign of peace. We say: **"Peace be with you."**

12

Fold on this line.

The Liturgy of the Word

We listen to two readings from the Bible, from the Old Testament and the New Testament. After each one, the reader says: "The word of the Lord." We answer: **"Thanks be to God."**

5

✁ Cut on this line.

Then the priest takes the cup of wine. He says: "Take this, all of you, and drink from it, for this is the chalice of my Blood. . . ."

10

We stand to say aloud what we believe as Catholics. Then we pray for the Church and all God's people. After each prayer we say: **"Lord, hear our prayer."**

7

We stand and sing Alleluia. The priest or deacon reads the Gospel. Then he says: "The Gospel of the Lord." We answer: **"Praise to you, Lord Jesus Christ."**

6

We sing or pray: **"Amen."** We believe Jesus Christ is really present in the Eucharist.

11

Fold on this line.

Cut on this line.

The Liturgy of the Eucharist

The priest prepares the altar. People bring gifts of bread and wine to the priest. The priest prepares these gifts. We pray: **"Blessed be God for ever."**

8

Then we remember what Jesus said and did at the Last Supper. The priest takes the bread. He says: "Take this, all of you, and eat of it, for this is my body, which will be given up for you."

9

Glossary

absolution (page 89) God's forgiveness of our sins, given by the priest in the Sacrament of Penance

Apostles (page 23) the twelve men that Jesus chose to lead his disciples

Baptism (page 79) the sacrament in which we receive God's sanctifying grace and become children of God and members of the Church

Beatitudes (page 112) teachings of Jesus that describe the way to live as his followers

bishops (page 56) leaders of the Church who carry on the work of the Apostles

Blessed Trinity (page 29) One God in Three Persons: God the Father, God the Son, and God the Holy Spirit

blessing (page 74) a sign of God's favor or a prayer asking God to make someone or something holy

Body of Christ (page 52) a way to describe the Church

Christ (page 31) the title given to Jesus that means he was God's chosen one

Church (page 24) all the people who are baptized in the name of the Blessed Trinity and are part of the Body of Christ

community (page 171) a group of people joined together by where they live or other things they have in common

confession (page 89) telling our sins to the priest in the Sacrament of Penance

Confirmation (page 80) the sacrament that seals us with the Gift of the Holy Spirit, who strengthens us to live our baptismal promises

conscience (pages 88, 113) God's gift that helps us to know right from wrong

contrition (page 89) being sorry for our sins and promising not to sin again

covenant (page 21) an agreement between God and his people

devotion (page 74) a form of personal or communal prayer

eternal life (page 40) living forever with God in the happiness of heaven

Eucharist (page 81) the sacrament in which we receive the Body and Blood of Jesus Christ

free will (page 106) God's gift of the freedom and ability to choose what to do

grace (page 65) God's life and love in us

Great Commandment (page 107) Jesus' teaching to love God, ourselves, and others

Holy Communion (page 81) receiving the Body and Blood of Christ

Holy Orders (page 95) the sacrament through which a baptized man becomes a bishop, priest, or deacon

Incarnation (page 45) the truth that the Son of God became man

justice (page 116) fair and respectful treatment of others

Kingdom of God (page 181) God's reign over sin, suffering, and death

Last Supper (page 81) the meal Jesus shared with his disciples on the night before he died, in which he gave us the Eucharist

liturgy (page 62) the official public prayer of the Church

Lord's Prayer (page 162) the prayer Jesus taught his followers

Mass (page 70) the celebration of the Eucharist

Matrimony (page 97) the sacrament in which a baptized man and baptized woman become husband and wife

mercy (page 90) God's love and forgiveness

mortal sins (page 131) sins that break our friendship with God

Original Sin (page 128) the first sin, which happened when the first man and woman, Adam and Eve, disobeyed God

Paschal Mystery (page 72) Christ's suffering, Death, Resurrection from the dead, and Ascension into heaven

penance (page 89) a prayer or kind act we do to repair the harm from our sins

pope (page 56) the leader of the Church who continues the work of Saint Peter

prayer (page 146) talking and listening to God

Precepts of the Church (page 123) laws to help us to know and fulfill our responsibilities as members of the Church

psalms (page 165) songs of praise from the Bible

repent (page 140) to turn away from sin

Resurrection (page 40) Jesus' rising from the dead

sacramentals (page 66) blessings, actions, and objects that help us respond to God's grace received in the sacraments

sacraments (page 64) special signs given to us by Jesus through which God shares his life and love with us

sacred (page 105) holy

sacrifice (page 82) a gift offered to God

saints (page 74) members of the Church who led holy lives and are happy with God forever in heaven

Sign of the Cross (page 30) a blessing prayer of the Church that shows our faith in God, the Blessed Trinity

sin (page 31) something we freely choose to do even though we know it is wrong

Ten Commandments (page 120) ten special laws God gave to his people

venial sins (page 131) sins that hurt our friendship with God

vices (page 131) bad habits that hurt our friendship with God and with one another

virtue (page 114) a good habit that helps us act as God wants us to

worship (page 156) an expression, or showing, of love and honor

Q: **What is the Bible?**

A: The Bible is the book that contains God's own Word. The most important writings in the Bible are about God's Divine Son, Jesus. Jesus teaches us how much God loves us. Jesus also teaches us that God wants us to love one another. *CCC, 104, 125*

Q: **What is the Church?**

The Church is a community of people who believe that Jesus is the Son of God. Jesus is the Head of the Church. The Church includes those who, through faith and Baptism, follow the teachings of Jesus and are governed by the bishops in union with the pope. *CCC, 752, 759, 1187*

Q: **Who were the Apostles?**

A: The Apostles were twelve men chosen by Jesus to lead his disciples. *CCC, 858*

Q: **What is the Blessed Trinity?**

A: The Blessed Trinity is the Three Persons in One God: God the Father, God the Son, and God the Holy Spirit. The Three Persons of the Blessed Trinity are unique but are one and the same God. *CCC, 254, 261*

Q: **What is sin?**

A: A sin is something we freely choose to do even though we know it is wrong. *CCC, 1871, 1850*

Q: **Why did God send his Son, Jesus?**

A: God wanted us to live forever with him in the happiness of heaven. That is why God sent his only Son, Jesus, to save us from sin and lead us to eternal life. *CCC, 457, 458, 1016, 1051, 1060*

CCC = Catechism of the Catholic Church

Q: **What is the Incarnation?**

A: The Incarnation is the truth that the Son of God became man. *CCC, 495, 509*

Q: **Who is the pope?**

A: The pope is the leader of the Church who continues the work of Saint Peter. *CCC, 882*

Q: **Who are the bishops?**

A: The bishops are leaders of the Church who carry on the work of the Apostles. *CCC, 881, 886*

Q: **What is the liturgy?**

A: The liturgy is the official public prayer of the Church. In the liturgy, the Church gives thanks and praise to God the Father, Son, and Holy Spirit. The Eucharist is at the center of the Church's liturgy. *CCC, 1110, 1111*

Q: **What are the sacraments?**

A: The sacraments are special signs given to us by Jesus through which God shares his life and love with us. The sacraments unite us to the love of the Blessed Trinity. *CCC, 1131*

Q: **What is the Mass?**

A: The Mass is the celebration of the Eucharist. It is the Church's greatest celebration. It is our most important liturgy. *CCC, 1382*

Q: **What is the Paschal Mystery?**

A: The Pascal Mystery is Christ's suffering, Death, Resurrection from the dead, and Ascension into heaven. *CCC, 654, 1085*

Q: **Who are the saints?**

A: The saints are members of the Church who led holy lives and are happy with God forever in heaven. *CCC, 828*

Q: Why does the Church honor Mary?

A: The Church honors Mary because she is the Mother of God's Son, Jesus, and she is the greatest of saints. *CCC*, 971

Q: What is Baptism?

A: Baptism is the sacrament in which we receive God's sanctifying grace and become children of God and members of the Church. *CCC*, 1212, 1213

Q: What is Confirmation?

A: Confirmation is the sacrament that seals us with the Gift of the Holy Spirit, who strengthens us to live our baptismal promises. *CCC*, 1303

Q: What is the Last Supper?

A: The Last Supper is the meal Jesus shared with his disciples on the night before he died, in which he gave us the Eucharist. *CCC*, 1323

Q: What is the Eucharist?

A: The Eucharist is the sacrament of the Body and Blood of Jesus Christ. *CCC*, 1322, 1323

Q: What is Holy Communion?

A: Holy Communion is the act of receiving the Body and Blood of Christ. *CCC*, 1355

Q: What is conscience?

A: Conscience is God's gift that helps us to know right from wrong. *CCC*, 1786–1778

Q: What is the Sacrament of Penance and Reconciliation?

A: The Sacrament of Penance and Reconciliation is the sacrament in which we receive God's forgiveness and peace. *CCC*, 1422, 1440

Q: What are the steps that are always part of the Sacrament of Penance and Reconciliation?

A: The steps are: contrition, confession, penance, and absolution. CCC, 1448

Q: What is Holy Orders?

A: Holy Orders is the sacrament through which a baptized man becomes a bishop, priest, or deacon. CCC, 1593

Q: What is the Sacrament of Matrimony?

A: The Sacrament of Matrimony is the sacrament in which a baptized man and baptized woman become husband and wife. CCC, 1660

Q: What is free will?

A: Free will is God's gift of the freedom and ability to choose what to do. CCC, 1745

Q: What are the Beatitudes?

A: The Beatitudes are teachings of Jesus that describe the way to live as his followers. Following the Beatitudes will give us happiness that lasts. CCC, 1725, 1726

Q: What is a virtue?

A: A virtue is a good habit that helps us act as God wants us to. Three important virtues God gives us are faith, hope, and charity. CCC, 1833, 1840–1842

Q: What are the Ten Commandments?

A: The Ten Commandments are ten laws God gave to his people. By following the Ten Commandments, we know how to love God, ourselves, and others. CCC, 1975, 1983

Q: **What is the Great Commandment?**

A: The Great Commandment is Jesus' teaching to love God, ourselves, and others. *CCC, 1985*

Q: **What are the Precepts of the Church?**

A: The Precepts of the Church are laws to help us to know and fulfill our responsibilities as members of the Church. *CCC, 2041*

Q: **What is Original Sin?**

A: Original Sin is the first sin, which happened when the first man and woman, Adam and Eve, disobeyed God. *CCC, 1714*

Q: **What is the difference between mortal and venial sins?**

A: Mortals sins are very serious and break our friendship with God. Venial sins are less serious and hurt our friendship with God. *CCC, 1874, 1875*

Q: **What is prayer?**

A: Prayer is talking and listening to God. When we pray, we lift our hearts and minds to God. *CCC, 2590*

Q: **What is the Lord's Prayer?**

A: The Lord's Prayer is the prayer that Jesus taught his followers. When we pray the Lord's Prayer, we praise God. We ask him to help us obey his commandments. *CCC, 2774, 2776*

Q: **What are psalms?**

A: Psalms are songs of praise from the Bible. *CCC, 2720*

Q: **What is the Kingdom of God?**

A: The Kingdom of God is God's reign over sin, suffering, and death. We believe that when God's Kingdom fully comes, all people will know and share in God's love and life forever. *CCC, 2857*

Q: What are the liturgical seasons?

A: The liturgical seasons are the seasons in the calendar year that celebrate special people and events in our Church. The liturgical seasons are Advent, Christmas, Ordinary Time, Lent, the Triduum, and Easter. *CCC, 1158–1173*

Q: What is Advent?

A: Advent is a season in the liturgical year that prepares us to celebrate the coming of Jesus Christ at Christmas. *CCC, 524*

Q: What do we celebrate at Christmas?

A: At Christmas we celebrate the birth of Jesus. We celebrate the Son of God becoming man. *CCC, 525, 526, 1171*

Q: What do we celebrate during Ordinary Time?

A: During Ordinary Time, we celebrate the whole life of Jesus, his Death, and his Resurrection. *CCC, 1163, 1168, 1172, 1173*

Q: What is Lent?

A: Lent is a season in the liturgical year in which we prepare to celebrate the Resurrection of Jesus Christ. Lent begins on Ash Wednesday and lasts forty days. *CCC, 1438*

Q: What is the Triduum?

A: The Triduum is the high point of the whole Church year. It is three especially sacred days in which we recall the Last Supper, the Death of Jesus on the Cross, and God raising Jesus from the dead. *CCC, 1168*

Q: What is Easter?

A: Easter is a season in the liturgical year in which we celebrate the Resurrection of Jesus Christ. The last day of the Easter season is Pentecost Sunday. *CCC, 1169*

Index